THE B CORP DECLARATION OF INTERDEPENDENCE

WE ENVISION A GLOBAL ECONOMY THAT USES BUSINESS AS A FORCE FOR GOOD. THIS ECONOMY IS COMPRISED OF A NEW TYPE OF CORPORATION – THE B CORPORATION – **WHICH IS PURPOSE-DRIVEN AND CREATES BENEFIT FOR ALL STAKEHOLDERS, NOT JUST SHAREHOLDERS.** AS B CORPORATIONS AND LEADERS OF THIS EMERGING ECONOMY, WE BELIEVE: **THAT WE MUST BE THE CHANGE WE SEEK IN THE WORLD.** THAT ALL BUSINESS OUGHT TO BE CONDUCTED AS IF PEOPLE AND PLACE MATTERED. **THAT, THROUGH THEIR PRODUCTS, PRACTICES, AND PROFITS, BUSINESSES SHOULD ASPIRE TO DO NO HARM AND BENEFIT ALL.** TO DO SO REQUIRES THAT WE ACT WITH THE UNDERSTANDING **THAT WE ARE EACH DEPENDENT UPON ANOTHER AND THUS RESPONSIBLE** FOR EACH OTHER AND FUTURE GENERATIONS.

T0265777

Praise for *The B Corp Handbook, Second Edition*

"*The B Corp Handbook* shows that an economic agenda that serves people's needs while respecting planetary boundaries is compatible with, and ultimately even necessary for, financial success."
—Paul Polman, CEO, Unilever

"Every business owner interested in creating a more diverse, equitable, and inclusive economy should read this book."
—Dawn Sherman, CEO, Native American Natural Foods

"In an increasingly complex world, big brands and companies are fundamentally challenged as to whose interests they really serve. We joined the B Corp movement because we are convinced that addressing this challenge directly is the best way to reinforce trust with our stakeholders."
—Emmanuel Faber, CEO, Danone

"The B Corp principles of social, environmental, and economic justice are deeply aligned with the mission and core values of our worker-owned cooperative."
—Adria Powell, CEO, Cooperative Home Care Associates

"Our holistic vision for the company centers around our clothing, mindful business practices, and support of every employee's purpose. Being a B Corp allows us to fulfill our purpose in a bold way with other like-minded companies. *The B Corp Handbook* serves as a guide for using business as a force for good."
—Eileen Fisher, founder and President, Eileen Fisher

"I hope that five years from now, ten years from now, we'll look back and say B Corporations were the start of the revolution. The existing paradigm isn't working anymore—this is the future."
—Yvon Chouinard, founder of Patagonia

"*The B Corp Handbook* provides an essential teaching resource in preparing the next generation of business leaders to build a more sustainable and inclusive economy."
—Jessica Thomas, Director, Business Sustainability Collaborative, North Carolina State University

"We became a Certified B Corp because it closely aligns with our purpose of empowering people to live more beautiful lives. B Corp also aligns with our Community Commerce model, which provides individuals with access to the resources and opportunities they need to add value to themselves, their families, and their community through reinvestment, entrepeneurship, women's empowerment, education, and wellness."
—Emmet Dennis, Chief Marketing Officer, Sundial Brands

"The second edition of *The B Corp Handbook* focuses on helping companies make progress on diversity, equity, and inclusion. The message is clear: don't just wait for economic justice; make it happen!"
—**Naomi Vickers, Chief Operating Officer, BLK Capital Management**

"I think B Corporations will make more profits than other types of companies."
—**Robert Shiller, winner of the 2013 Nobel Prize in Economics and Professor of Economics, Yale University**

"*The B Corp Handbook* shows how using business as a force for good, not just pursuing short-term profits, can be better for consumers, employees, local communities, the environment, *and* your company's long-term bottom line."
—**Tony Hsieh, *New York Times* bestselling author of *Delivering Happiness* and CEO, Zappos.com**

"B Corporations recast the goals of the traditional business enterprise. They are becoming more prevalent as a new breed of businessperson seeks purpose with the fervor that traditional economic theory says entrepreneurs seek profit."
—**Daniel Pink, *New York Times* bestselling author of *When* and *Drive***

"*The B Corp Handbook* proves that any company can be pro-community, pro-business, and pro-environment—at the same time. Ryan Honeyman and Tiffany Jana show that there does not have to be any tradeoff between profitability and creating positive social change."
—**Suzanne DiBianca, Executive Vice President of Corporate Relations and Chief Philanthropy Officer, Salesforce**

"A must-read for every for-profit enterprise that aims to create social impact."
—**Cathy Clark, Adjunct Professor and Director, CASE i3, Fuqua School of Business, Duke University**

"In contrast to the plethora of books that discuss only the problems facing society, *The B Corp Handbook* offers a concrete, positive, market-based, and scalable systemic solution to addressing our greatest social and environmental challenges."
—**Marshall Goldsmith, *New York Times* bestselling author of *What Got You Here Won't Get You There***

Second Edition

NEW Tools for Building an Inclusive Economy

The
B Corp
Handbook

How You Can Use Business as a Force for Good

Ryan Honeyman and Tiffany Jana

Foreword by Rose Marcario, CEO, Patagonia

BK

Berrett–Koehler Publishers, Inc.

Berrett-Koehler Publishers, Inc.
1333 Broadway, Suite 1000
Oakland, CA 94612-1921
Tel: (510) 817-2277
Fax: (510) 817-2278
www.bkconnection.com

ORDERING INFORMATION
Quantity sales. Special discounts are available on quantity purchases by corporations, associations, and others. For details, contact the "Special Sales Department" at the Berrett-Koehler address above.
Individual sales. Berrett-Koehler publications are available through most bookstores. They can also be ordered directly from Berrett-Koehler: Tel: (800) 929-2929; Fax: (802) 864-7626; www.bkconnection.com.
Orders for college textbook / course adoption use. Please contact Berrett-Koehler: Tel: (800) 929-2929; Fax: (802) 864-7626.

Distributed to the U.S. trade and internationally by Penguin Random House Publisher Services.

Berrett-Koehler and the BK logo are registered trademarks of Berrett-Koehler Publishers, Inc.

Printed in Canada

Berrett-Koehler books are printed on long-lasting acid-free paper. When it is available, we choose paper that has been manufactured by environmentally responsible processes. These may include using trees grown in sustainable forests, incorporating recycled paper, minimizing chlorine in bleaching, or recycling the energy produced at the paper mill.

Library of Congress Cataloging-in-Publication Data

Names: Honeyman, Ryan, author. | Jana, Tiffany, author.
Title: The B corp handbook, second edition : how you can use business as a
   force for good / Ryan Honeyman, Tiffany Jana; foreword by Rose
   Marcario.
Description: Second Edition. | Oakland, CA : Berrett-Koehler Publishers,
   2019. | Revised edition of The B corp handbook, [2014]
Identifiers: LCCN 2018058751 | ISBN 9781523097531 (paperback)
Subjects: LCSH: Social responsibility of business. | Social entrepreneurship.
   | BISAC: BUSINESS & ECONOMICS / Entrepreneurship. | BUSINESS & ECONOMICS /
   Green Business.
Classification: LCC HD60 .H655 2019 | DDC 658.4/08--dc23
LC record available at https://lccn.loc.gov/2018058751

Second Edition
25 24 23 22   10 9 8 7 6 5 4 3

Cover Design and Illustration: Jerrod Modica, B Lab
Cover Producer: Daniel Tesser, Studio Carnelian
Interior design and composition: Seventeenth Street Studios
Copy editing: Todd Manza
Index: Richard Evans
Photo credits: see page 215

To the B Corp Community

CONTENTS

B Corps in Their Own Words

One of the most powerful aspects of this book is the opportunity to hear directly from the B Corp community—in its own words—about the benefits, challenges, and surprises of becoming a Certified B Corporation and using business as a force for good. Throughout the book you will find twenty B Corp Q&As with CEOs, executives, impact investors, and others from the following companies, big and small, from around the world:

Dawn Sherman, Native American Natural Foods—USA
(page 17)

Anton Espira, ECO2LIBRIUM—Kenya
(page 27)

Emmanuel Faber, Danone—France
(page 33)

Mele-Ane Havea, Small Giants—Australia
(page 42)

Cheryl Pinto, Ben & Jerry's—USA
(page 50)

Eloisa Silva, Mercado Birus—Chile
(page 57)

Adria Powell, Cooperative Home Care Associates—USA
(page 69)

EILEEN
FISHER

Eileen Fisher, Eileen Fisher—USA
(page 81)

FOREWORD

Patagonia was proud to become both a Certified B Corporation and a benefit corporation in January 2012. Becoming a Certified B Corporation meant we had successfully met rigorous standards of social and environmental performance, accountability, and transparency. Becoming a benefit corporation meant that we had enshrined our most deeply held social and environmental values in our business charter and articles of incorporation—and committed to specific practices based on those values for as long as we are in business. Indeed, our founder, Yvon Chouinard, stood first in line to sign the papers on the day the new benefit corporation law took effect in California. (There will be more on the similarities and differences between Certified B Corps and benefit corps later in this book.)

An important upside, one we didn't expect, has emerged from the recurring assessment process that is necessary to becoming a Certified B Corporation. Although we submit to other audits of labor and environmental practices, the B Impact Assessment (a free tool that helps companies measure, compare, and improve their social and environmental performance) provides us the only comprehensive view of our standing with all our stakeholders: owners, employees, customers, local communities, suppliers' communities, and the planet. The B Impact Assessment helps us keep our eye on the North Star by letting us know where we have improved and where we fall short—and need to dig in. Our 2012 assessment, for example, revealed much work to be done to improve our positive engagement in our communities. By 2016, thanks largely to our introduction of Fairtrade certified labor for much of our product line, community engagement had become a strong contributor to our total score.

Another benefit, one we did expect, has been the good company of like-minded businesses committed to serving the common good. We are so happy to see so many new faces each year. We are impressed at how the movement has grown, both geographically and in the types and sizes of businesses involved. The informal communications between Certified B Corps on shared challenges and practices may be one of the movement's greatest benefits. The B Corp community is looking at the whole picture and planning longer term, which leads to innovation, thoughtful initiatives, and increased trust among stakeholders.

Ryan Honeyman wrote the original comprehensive B Corp Handbook that helped spark the growth of this movement. This second, expanded and updated edition, written with co-author Dr. Tiffany Jana, reflects much of what has changed and what we have all learned in the years since the first book appeared. Especially welcome in the second edition is the emphasis on diversity, equity, and inclusion, which will be helpful to us at Patagonia to continually improve our organization and to help support groups working for environmental justice around the world.

We live in a time of great injustice, political upheaval, and unparalleled threats to the web of life, but also of urgency, humility, and great opportunity to get things right and make things right. Ryan and Dr. Jana, in this book, help guide the way.

Rose Marcario
Chief Executive Officer, Patagonia Inc.

INTRODUCTION

Ryan Honeyman
(pronouns: he/him/his)

I first found out about B Corporations while baking cookies. The flour I was using—King Arthur unbleached all-purpose flour—had a Certified B Corporation logo on the side of the package. "That seems silly," I thought. "Wouldn't you want to be an A Corporation and not a B Corporation?" The carton of eggs I was using was rated AA. I was obviously missing something.

An online search revealed that the B logo was not a scarlet letter for second-rate baking product. B Corporations, I found, were part of a dynamic and exciting movement to redefine success in business by using their innovation, speed, and capacity for growth not only to make money but also to help alleviate poverty, build stronger communities, restore the environment, and inspire us to work for a higher purpose. The B stands for "benefit," and as a community, B Corporations want to build a new sector of the economy in which the race to the top isn't to be the best in the world but to be the best for the world.

Since my initial discovery, I have watched the B Corp movement grow to thousands of businesses in over sixty countries. In addition to King Arthur Flour, well-known B Corps include Ben & Jerry's, Danone North America, Eileen Fisher, Kickstarter, Laureate Education, Method, Natura, Patagonia, Seventh Generation, and Triodos Bank. Thought leaders such as former President Bill Clinton and Robert Shiller, the winner of the Nobel Prize in economics, have taken an interest in the B Corp movement. Inc. magazine has called B Corp certification "the highest standard for socially responsible businesses," and the New York Times has said, "B Corp provides what is lacking elsewhere: proof."[1]

> *You ought to look at these B Corporations. . . . We've got to get back to a stakeholder society that doesn't give one class of stakeholders an inordinate advantage over others.*
>
> Bill Clinton, former president of the United States

> *I think B Corporations will make more profits than other types of companies.*
>
> Robert Shiller, Nobel laureate in economics

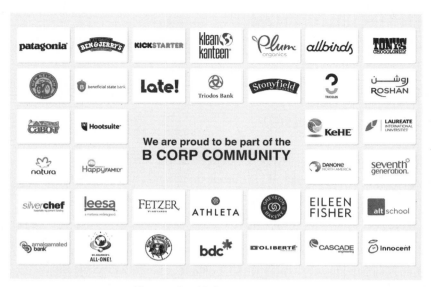

MEET SOME OF THE B CORPS. Thousands of B Corps across more than sixty countries are leading a movement to redefine success in business.

I originally decided to write this book because many business owners and CEOs are intrigued and excited by the idea of B Corporations but there was not a single step-by-step resource that could explain the what, why, and how of the B Corp movement. There was a need for a book that was practical and hands-on, a comprehensive guide for those interested in using business as a force for good.

The main focus of this book is the Certified B Corporation, not the legal entity known as a benefit corporation. This book focuses on the Certified B Corporation because this certification (and the B Impact Assessment, the free online tool for improving a company's social and environmental performance) is available to any business in the world, regardless of existing legal structure, size, or location of incorporation. There is a separate book written on benefit corporations, *Benefit Corporation Law and Governance: Pursuing Profit with Purpose*, by Frederick Alexander. I highly recommend it for those of you who want to go deep on the topic. For some of the basics, you may review appendix A of this book for an overview of benefit corporations, answers to some frequently asked questions about the legal structure, and a look at the similarities and differences between Certified B Corporations and benefit corporations.

This second edition of *The B Corp Handbook*, which I have coauthored with Dr. Tiffany Jana of TMI Consulting, updates the core content from the first edition of the book while adding Dr. Jana's expertise on diversity, equity, and building a more inclusive economy.

A lot has changed for me since 2014, when the first edition of this book was written. I now have two kids, a girl and a boy. Any parent reading this knows that something changes when you have kids. For me, having a girl made me viscerally aware of the many systemic barriers she will face in this world. It made me feel sad, angry, and helpless. Her birth caused the first in a series of deeper revelations. For example, many ideas that I was intellectually supportive of—like women's empowerment—suddenly became personal and real.

In addition to being a new father, this shift inside of me was accelerated by watching more cell phone videos of the police shooting unarmed black men, by Indigenous-led protests against the Dakota Access Pipeline, by the power of the #MeToo movement, or by immigrant children being forcibly separated from their parents just for seeking a better life in the United States. The confluence of these events reordered my internal list of personal and professional priorities. Diversity, equity, and inclusion (DEI) shifted from one of many issues I care about to my top priority.

This book is a lot different than the first edition. Some readers may have mixed reactions to the addition of so much content around DEI. You might think, "I wanted to read a straightforward book about B Corps, and you are blindsiding me with all of this DEI content. It feels like you are forcing this topic on readers when it is just one of many priorities. If I wanted to read a book about diversity, I would get one."

If you find yourself thinking along these lines, I understand the reaction. I may have thought the exact same thing before 2014. What I have learned over the past few years, however, is that there is no such thing as a conversation about DEI and a separate conversation about business as a force for good. They are the same conversation. Siloing DEI into something separate is one of the main barriers facing our movement to create a more equitable society.

Another thing I have learned is that, as a cisgender (that is, my gender identity matches the sex I was assigned at birth), nondisabled, straight, white male who is a U.S. citizen, it is the privilege of people like me to *not* think about DEI. We can mostly ignore it, or expect people of color (or other historically marginalized groups) to figure it out, or we can indefinitely kick the conversation down the road without any apparent negative repercussions. It should not be the burden of people of color, women, or other marginalized groups to educate folks with privilege about institutional racism, institutional sexism, and other forms of systemic bias.

One reason privileged people like me avoid this topic is that many of us feel like we don't know where to start—even if we are interested in addressing systemic bias. Another reason is that conversations about DEI, especially about race, often bring up feelings of shame, guilt, hopelessness, anger, and sadness. I have taken solace in the advice I have received from racial justice educators and social justice activists over the last few years. Their comments have generally followed along the lines of the following:

- "Yes, you are a privileged white male. However, you did not invent racism, sexism, and other forms institutional oppression. You inherited them."
- "It is OK to feel awkward and uncomfortable when talking about DEI. Try to stay engaged. If you choose to walk away from an uncomfortable conversation, you are exercising your privilege, because people of color, women, and others cannot walk away from their identity."
- "Do not doubt that you will make mistakes and feel embarrassed. Perfection is not the goal. Stay engaged long enough to give yourself a chance to recover from your mistakes, make a breakthrough in understanding, and strengthen your ability to have difficult conversations."

If it feels awkward and uncomfortable to talk about DEI, it can be absolutely terrifying to discuss white supremacy. "Whoa, whoa, whoa," I can hear you saying. "Are you seriously bringing up white supremacy in the introduction to a book about B Corps? I am about to throw this book out the window." If you are having this reaction, I get it. Hang in there. I promise this will tie back to B Corps.

As a white person (or for any person, for that matter), the term "white supremacy" is often jarring and cringeworthy. It can conjure up images of neo-Nazis and Ku Klux Klan members marching down the street with torches—leading to feelings such as shame, defensiveness, or anger. However, I am not proposing that we discuss the bigotry of individuals who identify as white supremacists. I want to examine the system or organizing principle of white supremacy, in which white domination of society is seen as the natural order of things. For white people like me, it is important to discuss this system, because it goes largely unnoticed and operates by default in the background of our daily lives.

"Again," you may be wondering, "how is this possibly related to B Corps? I don't see the connection." It is related because our economy is based upon—and tightly intertwined with—the legacy of white supremacy. If we aren't directly learning about, disrupting, and dismantling this framework, how can B Corps be truly successful in creating a more inclusive economy?

After learning more about this system from leaders in the antiracism movement, I believe it is important to specifically name white supremacy in the context of the B Corp movement because white supremacy is the system that perpetuates many of the problems our diversity, equity, and inclusion initiatives are attempting to solve. For instance, white supremacy implies a number of unspoken norms. It describes a social order in which one kind of person is superior: a white, Anglo, cisgender, Christian, heterosexual, wealth-oriented, nondisabled male. People who do not fit neatly into each of these categories and who want access to power and privilege are often forced to Anglicize their names, hide their sexuality, play up their wealth, act "male," and hide their religion.

The culture of white supremacy also elevates a certain attitude and approach to life. Many of the values I learned and internalized growing up as a young white male included things like, "Work hard. Keep your nose to the grindstone. Be productive. If you see a problem, fix it. You can do anything you want if you just try hard enough. Everyone gets a fair shot. You are responsible for your own success in life. Suck it up and don't complain. Always be polite. Avoid conflict. Don't rock the boat. If you don't have anything nice to say, don't say anything at all." For years, I assumed that the values imparted to me by my family were somehow unique to us. It shocked me to realize that these messages are part of a cultural lineage and belief system that is handed down by white families to their children over many generations.

These internalized values play out in subtle and pernicious ways. For example, if a white child sees a poor black child at school, they might think, "Well, maybe their family just needs to work harder," or "We should help those poor people, who obviously haven't figured it out and need the assistance of people like me." Based on the narrative that everyone gets a fair chance and that working hard is the answer, the white child may assume that the black child's family is solely responsible for the circumstances in which they find themselves. In addition, white children are taught to avoid conflict. "I'm confused why this black child is poor," the white child might think, "but I'm not going to ask about it. It seems like a sensitive topic. It must just be the way things are."

Nothing in the previous example was consciously or purposefully racist on the part of the white child. If anything, the white child thought they could be helpful. The cause of the damaging conclusions is the unexamined belief system—the default order of things—that has been passed down to white people and that perpetuates institutional bias.

Until recently, I had always believed that the answer to many social and environmental problems was to "help" historically marginalized groups bring themselves up to par with white communities. I had never considered that challenging and unraveling the norms, assumptions, and culture of white supremacy itself could be part of the solution. Reframing this problem is difficult and uncomfortable because it shifts the focus to me. That is why I believe it is incumbent upon us in the B Corp community to more explicitly name white supremacy and examine its negative effects. Antiracist leaders have helped me to understand that only by naming it, disrupting it, and dismantling it can we successfully create an economy that works for the benefit of all life.

Two things became readily apparent in deciding to incorporate DEI into this book. First, it was clear that, as a white male with all of the socially accepted and normative characteristics I have just mentioned, I was not the right person to lead a discussion about inclusion. I needed the help of an expert. Second, I strongly felt that DEI should not be a case study, featured section, or stand-alone chapter. It should touch every aspect of the book. Dr. Tiffany Jana was the first person that came to mind.

I have known and admired Dr. Jana for many years. They are a B Corp CEO, an expert on DEI, a doctor of management and organizational leadership, and an international public speaker. They are the coauthor of *Overcoming Bias: Building Authentic Relationships Across Differences* (Berrett-Koehler 2016) and *Erasing Institutional Bias: How to Create Systemic Change for Organizational Inclusion* (Berrett-Koehler 2018). I am incredibly lucky to have Dr. Jana as a coauthor of this book. In fact, I'll stop gushing about Dr. Jana and let them take it from here.

Dr. Tiffany Jana
(pronouns: they/them/theirs)

I was thrilled to be invited to coauthor the second edition of this book, because it reinforced something I already knew. Namely, that the B Corp community, by and large, seeks greater diversity among and within its businesses. Ryan's invitation registered as a fantastic opportunity to share what I have learned about expanding inclusion, designing equitable systems, and increasing diversity within communities. DEI is not just a vocation for me. It's a deeply personal calling.

There is an unexpected backstory to this book that reflects the depth of change I have witnessed on a personal, professional, and societal level. When Ryan first reached out to me, in the fall of 2017, I identified as a woman and was married to a white antiracist. Neither of those is true anymore. In addition to no longer being with my former partner and to subsequently deepening my connection to communities of color, I also now identify as a gender-nonconforming Christian. This means, among other things, that my pronouns have shifted from she/her/hers to they/them/theirs. As a Christian, the singular/plural God construct of the Holy Trinity is accessible to me. The idea that God, as "they," is part of me is as important as when I use the gender-nonconforming aspect of "they." It's a constant reminder that I am not just one thing.

The level of urgency I feel about DEI has evolved as well. When Ryan and I first spoke about the book, I was still grounded in my personal and professional experience as a global citizen. I was happy to moderate my voice in order to appeal to people as gently as possible. Being married to a cisgendered, white male helped me embody racial reconciliation on a daily basis. It also helped me to whitewash my life and enjoy a level of privilege that stands in stark contrast to the experiences of many of my brothers and sisters of color. My credit score went through the roof. I wasn't pulled over once during the seven years we were married—if he was driving. I was taken more seriously when I brought him to business functions, whether he contributed or not. While this approach has served me well (benefiting from pro-white bias and being white adjacent), I am not sure it still does, going forward.

Now is not the time for me to get comfortable, tread lightly, and sidestep the tough conversations. Racism, sexism, homophobia, ableism, and the legacy of white supremacy, slavery, and institutionalized bias are real and continue to wreak havoc in our communities. The blacker, poorer, and more marginalized you are, the worse the disparities. It is time that we, as citizens of the world and especially as B Corps, get real about what's going on.

In the time that it took to complete this book, there was an enormous shift across the world. Nationalism (especially white nationalism) has increased in the United States, Europe, and other countries and regions. Civil rights, and the progress toward equality many of us believed we had made, have been eroded. Classism is costing the poor (of all races and ethnicities) even more freedom and opportunity. Puerto Rico remains isolated in devastation after a natural disaster that likely would have been addressed more quickly and effectively had its population been more white and affluent. An increasing number of unarmed African American men, women, and children are being harassed, abused, and killed on video, with seemingly no justice for their abusers and killers. People are being sentenced for unreasonable lengths of time for nonviolent crimes and subsequently are subjected to inhumane conditions that most people are oblivious to or do not care about.

You may wonder what any of this has to do with B Corps. Well, everything. The B Corp community has placed a flag in the ground stating that we are here in service of the earth and her inhabitants. If we fail to leverage our collective economic power to address what we can clearly see are gross injustices—economic, environmental, social, medical, educational, and more—then are we really walking the walk?

Remember, DEI is not just an American thing. DEI is a global phenomenon. The difference is the type of diversity and who has been or is being marginalized. There is always a subset of people who are treated less than fairly. Humans are prone to the marginalization of others based on fear of differences that they don't accept or understand. In the United States, for instance, racial divides are the source of much conflict. Despite the fact that ethnic minorities in the United States are called "people of color," we are in fact "people of the global majority."

Diversity is always relative. In other countries, race may not be the primary focus for discrimination. People around the world are marginalized for their religion, gender, sexual orientation, disability, citizenship status, or low income.

I understand that conversations about DEI can make some people really uncomfortable. It can be frightening to discuss this topic if you feel ill-equipped to navigate the perilous waters of conversations about equity. Rather than avoiding this topic indefinitely, my advice is to be gentle on yourself and others. Everyone has to learn how to navigate hard conversations. As a DEI practitioner, I still have to learn, read, study, process, try, fail, blunder, and recover along my journey. I have used dated terminology that people find insulting. I have inadvertently privileged my temporarily able-bodied status. I've supported the gender binary construct without thinking. All of this was just in the last year. There are no perfect role models for DEI. We all mess up sometimes. It's usually just a matter of who is around when it happens and whether you are brave enough to own it and hold yourself accountable.

The important thing is to acknowledge your error, apologize whenever possible, and be more present and intentional next time. It takes practice, but cultural fluency is worth it. It is better to keep trying and to mess up than to be blindsided without any skills to employ. Take responsibility for your own understanding so your words and actions can reflect the thoughtful consideration of your fellow humans. With that in mind, let's briefly define what diversity, equity, and inclusion actually mean, since they are referenced frequently in this book.

- **Diversity** describes the differences among people, both demographic (race, ethnicity, gender, religion, class, age, and so on) and experiential (how people think, work, communicate, and live).

- **Equity** is often confused with equality. The difference between the two is important. Equality means everyone gets treated the same. Equity, on the other hand, means everyone gets treated according to their individual need or circumstances.

- **Inclusion** is the space we make for people to participate in systems. We can have all types of diversity, but if we fail to invite people to the table and empower them, they remain marginal. Inclusion means inviting people to join, participate fully, and help shape systems and make decisions. If you use people as tools to get work done but don't engage their minds and hearts, that is not inclusion. If people's opinions are not sought out, taken seriously, or acted upon, that is not inclusion. Inclusion is sharing the work, the opportunities, the glory, the fun, and the failure. Inclusion is rooted in welcoming people as they are and helping them grow and participate fully.

Our businesses are powerful tools that we can use to help build the world in which we want to live. This will require listening to those who are disenfranchised by systemic forms of oppression. People who have been exploited by our current economic system exist across the political spectrum, in rural and urban communities, around the world. In order to restore trust in business, the business community needs to respond to those people's legitimate desire for jobs with dignity. The business community also needs to make the case that economic justice for all is inextricably tied to, and dependent on, social and environmental justice.

You may be wondering what an inclusive economy actually looks like. An inclusive economy looks like a living wage for all workers. An inclusive economy looks like a boardroom and management team with the same demographics as the company's factory floor. An inclusive economy looks like ownership opportunities for all employees—especially historically marginalized groups like women and people of color. An inclusive economy holds institutions accountable for reinforcing racist, sexist, and other inequitable structures.

Systemic bias should not be nurtured or defended. Companies that thrive on the exploitation of people should not thrive. We can create an economy where inclusion and accountability are rewarded. The realization of these ideas should not depend solely on government regulation. They can be achieved through the leadership and stewardship of the business community, if we choose to take action.

As you will learn later in this book, one way for you to take the next step in building a more equitable economy is to try benchmarking your company's performance with the B Impact Assessment. The B Impact Assessment measures inclusive values that can help you quantify and shape the way you treat employees, your suppliers, local community members, and more. Completing the assessment will provide you with suggestions for creating substantive and impactful opportunities for individuals from chronically marginalized backgrounds. It also provides guardrails against some of the more tokenistic and superficial gestures that will fail to yield meaningful results.

The B Impact Assessment credits your business for supplier diversity, for creating equitable compensation structures, for investing in diverse recruitment, and for creating meaningful professional development opportunities. In addition, you are asked whether you pay a living wage, to measure pay differentials across your organization, and whether you provide scheduling flexibility for workers. Another consideration is the demographic composition of your staff, leadership team, and board of directors. If you do not have a board of directors, you will be invited to consider diversity, equity, and inclusion when the time comes to create one.

This is the magic of the B Corp journey. Your company may not be as equitable as you want it to be, but the B Corp movement provides the framework, tools, and community of support you need to continue to improve.

As you read this book, look for "Dr. Jana's Tips," where I describe practical solutions, metrics, suggestions, and best practices for the creation of a more inclusive economy. Whether you are part of an established B Corp or are still considering joining the movement, *The B Corp Handbook* will help you design a business that places diversity, equity, and inclusion in the foreground.

Part 1 of this book provides a brief history of the B Corp movement, a description of what B Corps are and why they are important, an overview of an emergent concept called the B Economy, a discussion about what investors think about B Corps, and an analysis of whether B Corp works for multinationals and publicly traded companies.

Part 2 goes into detail about the different benefits of becoming a Certified B Corporation—including joining a global community of leaders, attracting and retaining talent, benchmarking and improving performance, and more.

The third part describes the B Impact Assessment, a comprehensive tool that helps turn the desire to use business as a force for good—including the desire to integrate DEI more deeply into your company—into a series of concrete, measurable, and actionable steps. This section is a great resource, whether you want to become a Certified B Corporation or you are unsure about becoming a B Corp but want a free tool to assess, compare, and implement improvements that are good for workers, the environment, communities, governance, and customers. Whichever path you choose, this section will give you the insight, resources, and best practices necessary to make the most of your efforts.

For those who are fired up and ready to go, the Quick Start Guide in the fourth part outlines a six-step action plan to help you move forward on your journey as efficiently and inclusively as possible. Like the section on the B Impact Assessment, the Quick Start Guide is designed to be useful both for businesses that want to become a Certified B Corporation and for companies that simply want to improve their social and environmental performance. Look for "Ryan's Tips," which will help you move through the B Impact Assessment and/or the B Corp certification process with maximum effectiveness.

In the final part, we delve into a discussion about the work still left to be done as a B Corp community as it relates to DEI. We believe that the B Corp community has made a lot of progress on DEI, but there is still a lot of work to do. We end the main content of the book by discussing what success for the B Corp movement might look like.

Importantly, the collective wisdom of the B Corp community is present throughout this book. More than two hundred CEOs, sustainability directors, impact investors, marketing executives, human resources directors, and others from an international cohort of Certified B Corporations submitted responses for this book. The goal was to get a wide range of opinions, directly from the B Corp community, about why they became a B Corp, the business benefits of B Corp certification, and the challenges that typically arise during the certification process. We also asked respondents to provide advice for companies that are considering whether to certify. In fact, one of the most powerful aspects of this book is the opportunity to hear fellow business leaders describe, in their own words, why their company became a B Corp and why they think B Corps matter.

There are three final things to consider. First, B Corp offers a framework that any company in any state or country in the world can use to build a stronger and more inclusive business. This framework is relevant whether you are a business-to-business (B2B) or a business-to-consumer (B2C) business, a local sole proprietor or a global brand, a start-up or a third-generation family business, a limited liability company or a partnership, an employee-owned company or a cooperative, a C corporation or an S corporation, or even if you are still deciding on the right structure for a new business.

Second, B Corp is relevant to you personally, whether you are attracted or repelled by such terms as "green," "socially responsible," or "sustainable"; whether you consider yourself conservative or progressive; whether you consider yourself an expert in DEI or a beginner; whether you are a student, a young entrepreneur, or an experienced businessperson. If you have ever thought about how you could make a living and make a difference, about how you can build a more equitable economy, about your legacy and the example you set for your kids, or about leading a purpose-driven life—and especially if you've thought about how you could use business as a force for good—the B Corp movement is for you.

Finally, DEI should not exist as a side project, an isolated initiative, or something your company talks about once every few years. B Corps and aspiring B Corps would be wise to integrate DEI into every aspect of their businesses. Addressing bias, racism, sexism, or any diversity challenge is not like surgery to remove an appendix. You don't just cut it out one day and then it's over. It's more like hygiene—you have to keep tending to it if you want to stay healthy.

The world is watching us. The B Corp community needs to continue to lead and inspire. After all, if B Corps can't get inclusion right, who can?

Developments in the B Corp Movement Since the First Edition

A lot of progress has been made since The *B Corp Handbook* was first published in 2014. Here are some of the major developments in the B Corp movement since then.

International Growth

There are now more Certified B Corps based outside than inside of the United States. There are Certified B Corps in more than sixty countries, including Afghanistan, Australia, Brazil, Chile, Kenya, Mongolia, the Netherlands, and Zambia (to name a few). This expansion is due, in large part, to the tireless work of B Lab (the nonprofit behind the B Corp movement) and its partners around the world. These global partners include B Lab U.S., B Lab Canada, Sistema B (Latin America),

GROWING THE GLOBAL MOVEMENT. Juan Pablo Larenas, cofounder and executive director of Sistema B, speaks about B Corporations to an audience in São Paulo, Brazil.

B Lab Australia and New Zealand, B Lab United Kingdom, B Lab Europe, B Lab Taiwan, B Lab East Africa, B Market Builders in Hong Kong and Korea, and the B Corp China team.

Private Equity/Venture Capital Investors

Mainstream investors are becoming much more receptive to the B Corp idea. For example, B Lab has collected publicly available information on more than $2 billion of investment in B Corps and benefit corporations by 150 different venture capital firms to date. Indeed, nearly every major Silicon Valley venture capital firm has invested in a Certified B Corporation and/or a benefit corporation. This includes Andreessen Horowitz, Benchmark Capital, Founders Fund, Goldman Sachs, Greylock Partners, GV (formerly Google Ventures), Kleiner Perkins, New Enterprise Associates, and Sequoia Capital.

Multinationals

Another important development has been growing interest of multinational organizations in the B Corp movement. For example, Danone, a $25 billion publicly traded food conglomerate, declared in 2017 that it seeks to become the first Fortune 500 company to earn B Corp certification. Danone has also certified nine of its subsidiaries as B Corporations. This includes Danone North America, which, at $6 billion in annual revenues, is the largest Certified B Corp in the world. Unilever, a $62 billion publicly traded consumer goods multinational, has recently made a number of B Corp acquisitions. From 2016 to 2017, Unilever acquired five Certified B Corps: Mãe Terra, Pukka Herbs, Seventh Generation, Sir Kensington's, and Sundial Brands. This was in addition to Ben & Jerry's, acquired by Unilever in 2000, which became a Certified B Corp in 2012. Natura, a Brazilian-based B Corp and leader in the cosmetics industry, made headlines when it acquired The Body Shop in 2017. This was the first billion-dollar acquisition by a B Corp—and it was a surprise to many people that a B Corp was the acquirer.

Public Markets

In 2017, Laureate Education, a higher education company with campuses around the world, was the first benefit corporation to have an initial public offering (IPO). Laureate Education was also the third Certified B Corporation to go public in the United States (behind former B Corps Rally Software and Etsy). Laureate, which was backed by the private equity firm Kohlberg Kravis Roberts, raised $490 million

PUBLICLY LISTED B CORPS. Tina Lo, vice chairwoman of O-Bank Group, a publicly traded B Corp bank in Taiwan, speaks to reporters at a B Corp event in Asia.

in its IPO. The company had previously closed a $383 million private equity pre-IPO round in 2016, which included Apollo Management, Kohlberg Kravis Roberts, and the Abraaj Group. Laureate Education going public is a big deal because many commentators were unsure about how the markets would react to a company that, as a benefit corporation, legally holds itself accountable to considering all stakeholders (students, workers, community, the environment, and others) when making decisions. Globally, other publicly traded B Corps currently include Australian Ethical, Murray River Organics, Silver Chef, and Vivid Technologies (in Australia); Natura (Brazil); Yash Papers (India); and O-Bank (Taiwan).

Benefit Corporation Governance

In a time of political gridlock, the B Corporation has generated bipartisan support across the globe. In the United States, legislation to create benefit corporations—a new corporate governance structure based on the B Corp idea—has been passed in "red" states like Louisiana and South Carolina, "blue" states like California and New York, swing states like Colorado and Pennsylvania, and even in Delaware, the home of corporate law, where more than 63 percent of Fortune 500 companies are incorporated. There are thousands of benefit corporations to date across 37 U.S. states, the District of Columbia, and Puerto Rico. Internationally, after being endorsed in 2014 by the G8 Social Impact Investment Task Force, benefit corporation laws have been passed in Italy and Colombia, with many other countries currently considering legislation. It is not hard to see why this idea receives bipartisan support. The benefit corporation legal structure and the B Corp certification are pro-business, pro-environment, pro-market, and pro-community.

Academia

When the first edition of *The B Corp Handbook* was published, in 2014, there were perhaps ten to twenty schools teaching about B Corporations. Now there are more than one thousand faculty members teaching about B Corps at more than five hundred colleges and universities—including the Federal University of Technology–Paraná, Harvard, the London School of Economics, MIT, North Carolina State University, Stanford, the University of Alberta, Yale, and other top academic institutions across the globe. It is clear that professors, students, and administrators around the world have recognized that in order to change the way we do business, we need to change the way we teach business. There are two formal networks of academics: the Global B Corp Academic Community and Academia B. The goal of these networks is to advance the state of academic study into business as a force for good.

Impact Management

We manage what we measure. This is one of the most basic truths in business. It follows that we ought to measure what matters most: the ability of a business to not only generate returns but also create value for its customers, employees, community, and the environment. To date, forty thousand companies have used the B Impact Assessment, a free tool that measures any company's overall social and environmental performance.

Bancolombia, the largest bank in Columbia and the third largest in Latin America, is a great example of a company that has used the B Impact Assessment to measure its impact beyond its own operations. For example, Bancolombia started using the B Impact Assessment to measure the social and environmental impacts of 150 of its key suppliers. The bank used the impact data to generate performance reports and highlight areas for improvement for suppliers who completed the assessment. Bancolombia envisions this as the first phase of a multiyear effort that they hope will eventually create deeper alignment and engagement with their more than thirteen thousand suppliers and one million customers throughout South America.

Another impact management tool that is becoming increasingly used is B Analytics. B Analytics is a flexible data platform that automatically aggregates and analyzes B Impact Assessment data. B Analytics is important because it allows investors, fund managers, nonprofits, and large corporations to accelerate change in the markets and to encourage change in their business communities. For instance, organizations like Ashoka, the Business Alliance for Local Living Economies, Conscious Capitalism, the Family Business Network, Social Capital Markets, and the Young Professionals Organization are helping companies in their network to measure and manage their positive impact.

"Best For" and "+ B" Campaigns

On a local level, B Lab has partnered with place-based leaders and local governments to create a series of "Best For" and "+ B" initiatives around the world. In 2015, the Best for NYC campaign encouraged all businesses in New York City to measure, compare, and improve their impact. The program was made possible by a coalition of partners, including community organizations, business and trade associations, universities, government agencies, banks, and large employers committed to supporting the local economy. Since then, other campaigns have included Best for Calais (France); Best for Geneva (Switzerland); Best for PDX (Portland, Oregon); Best for PHL (Philadelphia); MZA + B (Mendoza, Argentina); RIO + B (Río de Janeiro, Brazil); and STGO + B (Santiago, Chile). More cities will be launching similar campaigns in the near future.

Inclusive Economy Challenge

B Lab launched the Inclusive Economy Challenge in 2016. The challenge is a call to action, encouraging the B Corp community to increase its collective positive impact by moving toward a more diverse and equitable economy. Each year, companies participating in the Inclusive Economy Challenge choose three or more goals from the Inclusive Economy Metric Set, a subset of B Impact Assessment questions that focuses on themes like supporting vulnerable workers, climate change mitigation, supplier screening, and corporate governance. In the first year, 175 companies participated in the challenge, collectively achieving 298 measurable inclusion goals. B Lab launched this challenge because they, like many B Corps, believe that our community's vision of a shared and durable prosperity is not possible without an inclusive economy.

Dawn Sherman,
Native American
Natural Foods—USA

Q: Why did you decide to become a B Corp?

A: The mission of Native American Natural Foods (NANF) is to return the buffalo to the land, lives, and economy of Indian people. Our company is located on the Pine Ridge Indian Reservation in South Dakota. Pine Ridge is home to the Oglala Lakota people. It is also the poorest place in the United States, has unemployment rates between 65 and 85 percent, and has the lowest life expectancy in the western hemisphere, outside of Haiti.

Our main product is the Tanka Bar. The Tanka Bar is based on a traditional Lakota recipe of dried buffalo meat and fruit. By returning one million buffalo to their native lands, we aim to restore the economic foundation of health and prosperity to more than forty thousand Indian people living on Pine Ridge. NANF was founded as a social enterprise with a vision of economic self-determination. Once we heard about B Corp certification, we knew it aligned with our vision and would be a great benefit to our company.

Q: What was your biggest surprise about becoming a B Corp?

A: Our biggest surprise was our initial score on the B Impact Assessment. We earned Best for the World status for a number of reasons, including our employee-ownership model, our socially responsible product, and the personal and professional development opportunities we offer our employees. We have also been pleasantly surprised by the collaborations we have had with fellow B Corps, as well as the exposure we have received, being part of the B Corp community.

In addition, B Lab realizes that the Inclusive Economy Challenge is only a start. There is a lot more for B Lab and the B Corp community to learn about DEI. Whether you are interested in becoming a Certified B Corporation or not, B Lab has created a set of relevant, practical, and helpful best practice guides that any company can use to build a more inclusive business. Visit bcorporation.net to download these guides and/or to learn more about the Inclusive Economy Challenge.

1

Overview

R yan first discovered the AND 1 mixtapes in the late 1990s. The mixtapes were a series of basketball "streetballing" videos, created by the popular basketball shoe and apparel company AND 1, that featured lightning-quick ball handling, acrobatic slam dunks, and jaw-dropping displays of individual talent. Ryan was a huge fan of the AND 1 mixtapes because the players used flashy, show-off moves that were very different from the more traditional style of basketball played in college or the NBA at the time. Ryan was so fascinated with the mixtapes that he even integrated them into his lesson plans when he worked as an English teacher in Zhejiang Province, China.

Many years later, Ryan was quite surprised to find out that AND 1's cofounders, Jay Coen Gilbert and Bart Houlahan, along with Andrew Kassoy, their longtime friend and former Wall Street private equity investor, were the people who created the Certified B Corporation. Ryan learned that Coen Gilbert's and Houlahan's experiences at AND 1, and Kassoy's experience on Wall Street, were central to their decision to get together to start B Lab, the nonprofit behind the B Corp movement.

AND 1 was a socially responsible business before the concept was well known, although AND 1 would not have identified with the term back then. AND 1's shoes weren't organic, local, or made from recycled tires, but the company had a basketball court at the office, on-site yoga classes, great parental leave benefits, and widely shared ownership of the company. Each year it gave 5 percent of its profits to local charities promoting high-quality urban education and youth leadership development. AND 1 also worked with its overseas factories to implement a best-in-class supplier code of conduct to ensure worker health and safety, fair wages, and professional development.

That was quite progressive for a basketball shoe company, especially because its target consumer was teenage basketball players, not conscious consumers with a large amount of disposable income. AND 1 was a company where employees were proud to work.

AND 1 was also successful financially. From a bootstrapped start-up in 1993 to modest revenues of $4 million in 1995, the company grew to more than $250 million in U.S. revenues by 2001. This meant that AND 1—in less than ten years—had risen to become the number two basketball shoe brand in the United States (behind Nike). As with many endeavors, however, success brought its own set of challenges.

AND 1 had taken on external investors in 1999. At the same time, the retail footwear and clothing industry was consolidating, which put pressure on AND 1's margins. To make matters worse, Nike decided to put AND 1 in its crosshairs at its annual global sales meeting. Not surprisingly, this combination of external forces and some internal miscues led to a dip in sales and AND 1's first-ever round of employee layoffs. After painfully getting the business back on track and considering their various options, Coen Gilbert, Houlahan, and their partners decided to put the company up for sale in 2005.

The results of the sale were immediate and difficult for Coen Gilbert and Houlahan to watch. Although the partners went into the sale process with eyes wide open, it was still heartbreaking for them to see all of the company's preexisting commitments to its employees, overseas workers, and local community stripped away within a few months of the sale.

The Search for "What's Next?"

In their journey from basketball (and Wall Street) to B Corps, Coen Gilbert, Houlahan, and Kassoy had a general sense of what they wanted to do next: the most good for as many people as possible for as long as possible. How this would manifest, however, was not initially clear.

Kassoy was increasingly inspired by his work with social entrepreneurs as a board member of Echoing Green (a private equity firm focused on social change) and the Freelancers Insurance Company (a future Certified B Corporation). Houlahan became inspired to develop best practices to support values-driven businesses that were seeking to raise capital, grow, and hold on to their socially and environmentally responsible missions. And Coen Gilbert, though proud of AND 1's culture and practices, wanted to go much further, inspired by the stories of iconic socially responsible brands such as Ben & Jerry's, Newman's Own, and Patagonia, whose organizing principle seemed to be how to use business for good.

The three men's initial, instinctive answer to the "What's next?" question was to create a new company. Although AND 1 had a lot to be proud of, they reasoned, the company hadn't been started with a specific intention to benefit society. What if they started a company with that intention? After discussing different approaches, however, Coen Gilbert, Houlahan, and Kassoy decided that they would be lucky to create a business as good as those created by existing social entrepreneurs such as Ahmed and Reem Rahim from Numi Organic Tea and Mike Hannigan and Sean Marx from Give Something Back Office Supplies. And more importantly, they decided that even if they could create such a business, one more business, no matter how big and effective, wouldn't make a dent in addressing the world's most pressing challenges.

They then thought about creating a social investment fund. Why build one company, they reasoned, when you could help build a dozen? That idea was also short lived. The three decided that even if they could be as effective as existing social venture funds such as Renewal Funds, RSF Social Finance, or SJF Ventures, a dozen fast-growing, innovative companies was still not adequate to address society's challenges on a large scale.

What Coen Gilbert, Houlahan, and Kassoy discovered, after speaking with hundreds of entrepreneurs, investors, and thought leaders, was the need for two new basic elements to accelerate the growth of—and amplify the voice of—the entire socially and environmentally responsible business sector. This existing community of leaders said they needed a legal framework to help them grow while maintaining their original mission and values, and credible standards to help them distinguish their businesses in a crowded marketplace, where so many seemed to be making claims about being a "good" company.

To that end, in 2006 Coen Gilbert, Houlahan, and Kassoy cofounded B Lab, a nonprofit organization that serves a global movement of people using business as a force for good. The B Lab team worked with many leading businesses, investors, and attorneys to create a comprehensive set of performance and legal requirements—and they started certifying the first B Corporations in 2007.

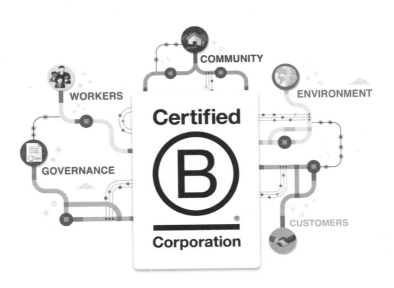

I often wonder to what extent business can help society in its goals to alleviate poverty, preserve ecosystems, and build strong communities and institutions. . . . B Lab has proven that there is a way.

Madeleine Albright, former U.S. Secretary of State

B Corps: A Quick Overview

Certified B Corporations are companies that have been certified by the nonprofit B Lab to have met rigorous standards of social and environmental performance, accountability, and transparency. B Corp certification is similar to Leadership in Energy and Environmental Design (LEED) certification for green buildings, Fairtrade certification for coffee, or USDA Organic certification for milk. A key difference, however, is that B Corp certification is of an entire company and its practices (such as worker engagement, community involvement, environmental footprint, governance structure, and customer relationships) rather than looking at just one aspect of a company (such as the building or a product). This big picture evaluation is important because it helps distinguish between good companies and just good marketing.

Today, there is a growing global community of thousands of Certified B Corporations across hundreds of industries working together toward one unifying goal: to redefine success in business so that one day all companies will compete not just to be the best *in* the world but also to be the best *for* the world.

When we first heard about the B Corp movement, we said, "That's what we've been trying to say and do this whole time!" It just fit with our approach and philosophy completely.

Alex Houlston, Energy for the People—Australia

As a quick overview, companies that wish to become Certified B Corporations must meet three basic requirements: verified social and environmental performance, legal accountability, and public transparency. Each of these steps, briefly outlined here, will be covered in more detail later in the book.

1. **Verified social and environmental performance.** To meet the performance requirement, a company must earn a minimum verified score of 80 points or above on the B Impact Assessment. The B Impact Assessment measures a company's overall impact on its workers, community, customers, and the environment.

2. **Legal accountability.** Certified B Corporations are legally required to consider the impact of their decisions on all their stakeholders. The legal requirement can be fulfilled through a variety of structures, from the limited liability company (LLC) and traditional corporations to benefit corporations and cooperatives.

3. **Public transparency.** Transparency builds trust. All Certified B Corps must share their B Impact Report publicly on bcorporation.net. The B Impact Report is the summary of a company's scores on the B Impact Assessment, by category, and contains no question-level information.

Nonprofits, such as 501(c)(3)s in the United States, and government agencies are not eligible to certify as B Corps. Companies with any of the following corporate structures may become Certified B Corps: benefit corporations, C corporations or S corporations, cooperatives, employee stock ownership plans, LLCs, low-profit limited liability companies (L3Cs), partnerships, sole proprietorships, wholly owned subsidiaries, or for-profit companies based outside the United States. This list is not exhaustive; see bcorporation.net for more details.

To finalize the B Corp certification process, prospective companies must sign the B Corp Declaration of Interdependence (a document outlining the values that define the B Corp community), sign a B Corp Agreement (a term sheet that defines the conditions and expectations of B Corp certification), and pay their annual certification fee (which is calculated based on a company's annual sales). The certification term for B Corps is three years. After three years, companies are required to complete an updated B Impact Assessment and go through the verification process again in order to maintain their certification.

THE B ECONOMY IS BIGGER THAN B CORPS. B Lab collaborates across all sectors of society to build a global movement of people using business as a force for good.

ECO₂LIBRIUM
Sustainable Solutions

Anton Espira,
ECO₂LIBRIUM—Kenya

Q: **What business benefits do you directly attribute to your B Corp certification?**

A: The most obvious benefit has been the recognition and attention we have received, particularly as one of the highest-scoring B Corps in the world, and as one of a few founding members of the B Lab East Africa movement. This gives us a lot of free publicity and helps in approaching partners, investors, and regulatory bodies. Beyond this, one of the most important benefits has been the huge morale boost our team has received from the knowledge that their work is relevant on a bigger stage than just the communities they work in. Being based in a small town in rural Kenya, one can feel isolated. The global recognition that comes with B Corp certification is a massive external validation.

Q: **What is your company doing to help build a more inclusive economy?**

A: Working in rural Africa, we have had to fit business processes to societal needs. As a matter of principle, we try to hire the underserved, sourcing our team locally (not just in Kenya but from the poor communities around us). In addition, over 70 percent of direct beneficiaries from our business ventures (partners, employees, and contractors) are women. We believe that, in a world where trade and commerce have long superseded diplomacy as the primary engines of global interaction, the opportunity is ripe for business to be the main force for good in society.

The Emergence of the B Economy

One of the key concepts to develop since the publication of the first edition of *The B Corp Handbook* is the emergence of the "B Economy." The B Economy is bigger than the community of Certified B Corps. For instance, the B Economy includes thousands of Certified B Corporations; thousands of benefit corporations; more than forty thousand companies that have used the B Impact Assessment to benchmark and improve their performance; the growing number of investors who are investing in Certified B Corps and benefit corporations; thousands of academics who are teaching about and conducting research on the B Corp movement; large companies that are using the assessment to improve the social and environmental performance of their company, their subsidiaries, and their suppliers; thousands of employees who work for any of the aforementioned enterprises; and millions of customers who buy from and support companies who are using business as a force for good.

The B Economy is important because it means that anyone—not just Certified B Corps—can participate in our broader movement. We will have succeeded when we no longer need a separate B Economy—just a global economy that aligns its activities toward creating a shared and durable prosperity for all.

What Do Investors Think about B Corps?

Many entrepreneurs want to know whether becoming a Certified B Corporation and/or a benefit corporation will hurt their ability to raise capital. The evidence says no. According to research compiled by B Lab, 120 venture capital firms have invested more than $2 billion in Certified B Corporations and benefit corporations.

For example, mainstream venture capitalists such as Andreessen Horowitz, GV, Kleiner Perkins, New Enterprise Associates, and Sequoia Capital have invested in Certified B Corporations. Union Square Ventures, a venture capital firm that invested in Kickstarter, says B Corps are appealing because the companies that produce the most stakeholder value over the next decade will also produce the best financial returns. Rick Alexander, head of legal policy at B Lab, has written, "Since nearly all B Corps are privately held companies, it would be reasonable to start by asking if venture capital firms invest in B Corps. They do. In fact, at this point, nearly every major Silicon Valley venture capital firm has invested in a B Corp."[1]

Our B Corp certification is very important to our investors. It helps validate that we are making progress towards our goal of improving the livelihood of agribusinesses in developing nations.

Gabriel Mwendwa, Pearl Capital Partners—Uganda

Some of the Investors in Certified B Corps

Investor	Certified B Corp
Kohlberg Kravis Roberts	Laureate Education
Andreessen Horowitz	Altschool
Goldman Sachs	Ripple Foods
Union Square Ventures	Kickstarter
Greylock Partners	Change.org
New Enterprise Associates	Cotopaxi
Red Sea Ventures	Allbirds
Investeco	Kuli Kuli
Sequoia Capital	Lemonade
Obvious Ventures	Olly
Kleiner Perkins	Recyclebank
Foundry Group	Schoolzilla
Collaborative Fund	Fishpeople
Draper Fisher Jurvetson	WaterSmart Software
Tin Shed Ventures	Bureo
Force for Good Fund	Spotlight: Girls
White Road Investments	Guayaki
Silicon Valley Bank	Singularity University
Builders Fund	Traditional Medicinals
FreshTracks Capital	SunCommon

Does B Corp Work for Multinationals and Publicly Traded Companies?

Large companies, including multinationals and publicly traded companies, have many opportunities to take part in the growing B Economy. Some of these pathways include becoming a Certified B Corporation, incorporating as a benefit corporation, helping promote the movement to others, and using the B Impact Assessment and/or B Analytics to encourage key stakeholders to improve their social and environmental performance.

Another path to getting involved with the B Economy is to acquire a B Corp subsidiary. For example, Unilever, the consumer goods multinational, has gone on a recent spate of B Corp acquisitions. In 2016 and 2017, Unilever acquired five different Certified B Corps, including Mãe Terra, Pukka Herbs, Seventh Generation,

Talking to Investors: Q&A with Adam Lowry of Ripple Foods

Q: **You have raised over $100 million in venture capital from well-known investors like GV, Goldman Sachs, and Khosla Ventures. Have your investors had any positive and/or negative reactions to Ripple being a benefit corporation?**

A: Positive! Most established firms are fully on board with, or exclusively investing in, companies that drive social and environmental good. They want those companies to be authentic—driving measurable results and being transparent about what they do and don't do well and, most importantly, building the capability of continuous improvement. I have never had a potential investor avoid making an investment in our company because we are a benefit corporation.

Q: **What sort of language, examples, or arguments have you found effective in helping investors get comfortable with the benefit corporation legal structure?**

A: The primary concern I hear is "Does this structure create any new or additional liabilities that a more traditional structure does not?" It helps to have at least a cursory understanding of shareholder provisions. When that is addressed, investors are generally very comfortable. If you need to go in depth, bring in a lawyer with expertise in that area. At times I have leaned on an attorney familiar with benefit corporation statute in order to answer more technical questions.

Q: **What advice do you have for entrepreneurs who may be uncertain about their ability to raise capital if they convert to a benefit corporation?**

A: I think it's a nonissue. If anything, being a benefit corporation helps in the fundraising process. But be prepared. Do your research to understand the legal differences between benefit corporations and other corporate forms, and don't be afraid to enlist some help to address a potential investor's concerns directly.

Q: **Do investors have any questions about exit/liquidity as it relates to benefit corporations?**

A: Liquidity is really the same with benefit corporations. That's dictated by the terms of the purchase agreements that investors sign. The key is not that you can't sell; it's that you can't sell out (compromise your mission for liquidity). I've seen some investors push back on that, but, the way I see it, that's a great litmus test of whether an investor really means it when they say they want to invest in sustainable businesses. I would question someone who pushes back on my benefit corporation and B Corp status. It might be a sign that they are not the right investment partner to have in the first place.

Sir Kensington's, and Sundial Brands. This was in addition to Ben & Jerry's, which was acquired by Unilever in 2000 and became a Certified B Corp in 2012.

Other large multinationals, such as Anheuser-Busch, the Campbell Soup Company, Coca-Cola, Group Danone, the Hain Celestial Group, Nestlé, Procter & Gamble, Rakuten, SC Johnson & Son, and Vina Concha y Toro have acquired Certified B Corp subsidiaries in recent years.

Large Companies with B Corp Subsidiaries

Parent Company	Certified B Corp Subsidiaries
Anheuser-Busch	4 Pines Brewing Company
Azimut Group	AZ Quest
BancoEstado	BancoEstado Microempresas, CajaVecina
Campbell Soup Company	Plum Organics, The Soulfull Project
Coca-Cola	Innocent Drinks
Fairfax Financial	The Redwoods Group
Gap	Athleta
Group Danone	Aguas Danone Argentina, Alpro, Danone AQUA Indonesia Danone Canada, Danone North America, Danone Spain, Danone UK, Earthbound Farm, Happy Family Brands, Les 2 Vaches
Kikkoman	Country Life
Lactalis	Stonyfield Farm
Land O'Lakes	Vermont Creamery
Nestlé	Essential Living Foods, Garden of Life
OppenheimerFunds Inc.	SNW Asset Management
Procter & Gamble	New Chapter
Rakuten	OverDrive
SC Johnson & Son	People Against Dirty (Method, Ecover)
The Hain Celestial Group	Ella's Kitchen UK
Unilever	Ben & Jerry's, Mãe Terra, Pukka Herbs, Seventh Generation, Sir Kensington's, Sundial Brands
Vina Concha y Toro	Fetzer Vineyards

When we look at any of our acquisitions, one of the main considerations is always whether it is a good fit to Unilever. We look for companies that have similar vision and values to ours. That is critical to success of the partnership. B Corp companies come with many of the attributes that fit with our long-term goals and our culture, and therefore it is no surprise that some of our recent acquisitions, such as Seventh Generation, Pukka Herbs and Teas, and Sir Kensington, have been B Corps.

Paul Polman, Unilever—United Kingdom

Danone is a great example of a publicly traded multinational that is heavily involved with the B Corp movement on multiple levels. At the company's 2017 annual shareholder meeting, Danone CEO Emmanuel Faber announced Danone's intention to become the first Fortune 500 company to earn B Corp certification. In addition, once Danone decided to get more involved with the B Corp movement, the organization started helping several of its subsidiaries make progress toward B Corp certification. By using the B Impact Assessment, Danone was able to determine which subsidiaries were ready to move toward certification and which first needed focused improvement work.

"The B Impact Assessment represents a set of demanding standards, which some of our businesses are able to meet already," explains Blandine Stefani, B Corp community director at Danone. "For some others, becoming a Certified B Corp is an ambition that will require some changes to their practices, with the support of B Lab." Through a cohort process facilitated by B Lab, the subsidiaries completed the B Impact Assessment together, allowing Danone to monitor their progress and improvement using B Lab's B Analytics tool. For a large company like Danone, the Impact Management Cohort made pursuing B Corp certification for subsidiaries easier, faster, and more transparent.

As of 2018, Danone has nine subsidiaries certified as B Corps, is making use of the benefit corporation legal structure in the United States, is assessing and educating more business units using B Lab's impact management tools, and is taking a leadership role to create more pathways for multinational engagement.

In an innovative approach tying the cost of capital to environmental, social, and governance benchmarks, Danone partnered with twelve leading global banks that agreed to lower their loan rates if Danone increases its verified positive impact in the world. The percentage of Danone's sales from Certified B Corp subsidiaries was one of the environmental, social, and governance measurements. In other words, the more they sell from subsidiaries that are B Corps, the lower their cost of capital.

DANONE
ONE PLANET. ONE HEALTH

Emmanuel Faber,
Danone—France

Q: Why did you decide to become a B Corp?

A: In an increasingly complex world, big brands and companies are fundamentally challenged as to whose interests they really serve. At Danone, we are convinced that addressing this issue in straight and simple terms is the best way for our brands and our company to reinforce trust with employees, consumers, partners, retailers, civil society, and governments. That is why we joined the B Corp movement. Our ambition to obtain this certification globally is an expression of our longtime commitment to sustainable business and to Danone's dual project of economic success and social progress.

Q: What was your biggest surprise about becoming a B Corp?

A: The energy that it drives in our teams. We currently have nine B Corp subsidiaries, meaning that nearly 30 percent of Danone's global sales are now covered by the B Corp certification. We started our journey less than three years ago, and Danone North America achieved its certification two years ahead of schedule. This is significant and reflects the internal enthusiasm towards our global B Corp ambition. One of my colleagues in Mexico recently told me "B Corp is a way for us—as a company—to be closer to what we aspire to be as individuals."

Q: Anything else you would like to mention?

A: Although Danone as a global entity is not yet certified as a B Corp, our ambition is to be the first large multinational to do so. To B or not to B Corp, that is no longer a question!

The deal on Danone's $2 billion syndicated credit facility was led by BNP Paribas and includes Barclays, Citibank, Crédit Agricole, HSBC, ING, JPMorgan, MUFG, Natixis, NatWest, Santander, and Société Générale. The result is that the heads of corporate and institutional banking for a dozen of the world's largest credit providers—notoriously the most fiscally conservative people in any boardroom—have affirmed that becoming a Certified B Corporation reduces risk and can help you save money.

2

Benefits of Becoming a B Corp

Several benefits of becoming a Certified B Corporation relate directly to you and your business. B Corp certification helps you attract and retain talent, distinguishes your business in a crowded market, and helps associate your brand with some of the most socially and environmentally responsible companies on the planet. The particular benefits most attractive to you will vary depending on your industry, your goals and objectives, and where you are in the life cycle of your business (at start-up, in a growth phase, planning for succession, and so on).

Ryan was most attracted to the quality of the community. When he found out that King Arthur Flour, Method, and Seventh Generation were Certified B Corporations, Ryan had no doubt that he was also going to certify his company. Ryan had found a group of like-minded, innovative, and dynamic entrepreneurs who shared his core values.

Networking with other B Corps will give you energy for months.

Susanne Koolhof, Re-Vive—Belgium

Dr. Jana was interested in attracting highly qualified, passionate, and values-aligned millennials. Dr. Jana noted that becoming a B Corp meant that they no longer had to search for high-potential staff. They were now coming to her. Whereas Ryan was most attracted to the community and Dr. Jana was most excited about attracting top talent, a consumer products company like Ben & Jerry's, Numi Organic Tea, or Preserve might find the marketing benefits to be the most valuable. This might include placing the Certified B Corporation logo on product packaging, participating in the B Corp ad campaign, or taking advantage of in-store retail partnerships. Other businesses might be interested in joining B Corp Peer Circles, where they can share best practices on diverse, equitable, and inclusive hiring practices. Patagonia was initially attracted to the idea of protecting its social and environmental mission after its founder, Yvon Chouinard, and his wife, Malinda, retired. It could be a combination of these reasons. It really depends on your situation.

The following section describes the benefits that the majority of B Corps cited as the most valuable. However, these benefits are not ranked in any particular order, so feel free to start with what seems most interesting and valuable to you.

BEST FOR THE WORLD. Caroline Wanjiku, CEO of Daproim Africa, accepts the Best for the World award from Global B Corp ambassador Marcello Palazzi at a B Corp event in Kenya.

- Being part of a global community of leaders.
- Attracting talent and engaging employees.
- Increasing credibility and building trust.
- Benchmarking and improving performance.
- Protecting a company's mission for the long term.
- Generating press and awareness.

Being Part of a Global Community of Leaders

The incredible value of the community itself came as a surprise for many B Corps. Many said that they were originally interested in becoming a Certified B Corporation in order to take advantage of the marketing benefits, to receive discounts on products and services, or to benchmark their social and environmental performance. But, almost universally, it has been the strength of the global community—and the sense of being part of something bigger than an individual business—that has become the most deeply fulfilling aspect of B Corp certification.

The positivity, collaboration, diversity of experience, innovation, and joy of being part of a global community that shares your core values and a clear sense of purpose is what inspires, motivates, and energizes B Corps to use their businesses as a force for good. The B Corp community benefits from a high level of trust, a focus on equity and belonging, and an entrepreneurial spark that is very powerful.

In many ways, the value of the B Corp community itself makes sense. The rigor of the B Corp certification process means that it takes serious dedication to complete, which helps to filter out businesses that are not truly committed to meeting high standards of performance, accountability, and transparency. The result is a passionate, highly innovative group of some of the most socially and environmentally conscious businesses on the planet.

While the B Corp movement started in the United States, it was never intended to remain an American phenomenon. Indeed, since the first edition of this book was published in 2014, there are now more B Corps based outside of the United States than inside. This is because using business as a force for good has global appeal. For example, whether you are a sole proprietor, a national brand, or global business with billions in sales, and whether your focus is on strengthening local communities, reducing global poverty, or addressing climate change, being part of a larger movement can help build collective voice, accelerate the adoption of standards, drive capital, help secure supportive public policies, and inspire consumers to change their behavior.

To give you a sense of the power of this international movement, we asked each of B Lab's global partners to give us a few highlights of some of their region's accomplishments. Note that the following is only a small sampling of highlights—visit the B Corporation website for more information on each region. Here are some of the big wins and key milestones from each global partner.

Sistema B (Latin America), established in 2012

- After initially starting in four countries—Argentina, Brazil, Chile, and Colombia—the B Corp movement has spread to fifteen countries in Latin America.

- Grupo Bancolombia, the largest bank in Colombia, launched the first Measure What Matters program in the region. The program's initial focus was to use the B Impact Assessment to measure and manage the social and environmental impacts of 150 of its key suppliers. Fifteen other large companies in Latin America are following suit.

- Natura Cosméticos, a publicly traded B Corp based in Brazil, acquired The Body Shop and Aesop, spreading the B Corp movement to seventy countries.

- Santiago, Chile; Mendoza, Argentina; and Río de Janeiro, Brazil, launched Cities + B initiatives that bring together businesses, universities, foundations, public institutions, entrepreneurs, and citizens to develop solutions to their region's most difficult social and environmental challenges. A key component of these ongoing initiatives is to encourage businesses in each city to measure, manage, and improve their impact with the B Impact Assessment.
- More than 2,500 people take part in the Multiplicadores B (or B Multipliers) program to help spread the B Corp movement in Latin America.
- Colombia became the third country (behind the United States and Italy) to pass benefit corporation legislation. Five other Latin American countries are currently debating benefit corporation legislation in parliament.

B Lab Australia and New Zealand, established 2014

- Australia has four Australian Stock Exchange–listed companies that are Certified B Corps: Australian Ethical Investments, Murray River Organics, Silver Chef, and Vivid Technology.
- In 2017, the first local B Corp Champions Retreat drew two hundred B Corp Leaders from across Australia and New Zealand.
- B Lab Australia and New Zealand have begun pioneering an ecosystem partnership model with various organizations (such as banks, utility companies, and universities) who want to join the movement and accelerate the growth of the B Economy.
- Benefit corporation legislation has attracted widespread support from across the business and legal communities and is currently being considered by the federal government.

We became a B Corp because we wanted to be in a community of like-minded, like-hearted people and to be part of a leading movement for positive change. As a certain African proverb goes, "If you want to go fast, go alone. If you want to go far, go together."

Zara Choy, Digital Storytellers—Australia

B Lab Canada, established 2015

- FlipGive became the first Certified B Corp outside the United States, in 2008.
- Business Development Bank of Canada became the first Crown corporation to certify as a B Corporation. The bank has dedicated staff resources to growing the B Corp movement, starting in Western Canada and scaling to include other regions.

Small Giants

Mele-Ane Havea, Small Giants—Australia

Q: Why did you decide to become a B Corp?

A: Small Giants was the first B Corporation in Australia. We certified in 2012. We were excited to join a global community of like-minded individuals who wanted to change the world through business. We were also energized by the idea of putting a (B) flag in the ground as a callout to the remarkable businesses in our region who shared our B Corp values. We hoped they would join us to build a B Corp movement in Australia and New Zealand.

Q: What was your biggest surprise about becoming a B Corp?

A: For me, personally, it is the friendship and love. When I first met the B Corp community in the United States, I came back to Australia and I said, "They all hug so much!" I'm totally up for that, but what I didn't realize was that I would make lifelong friendships and connections from those hugs. The community is built on relationships, and the relationships are strong.

I say "love" because it is through our Sistema B brothers and sisters— the Empresa Bs in Latin America—that I first heard the word "love" thrown around in a business context. There were grown men talking about their love for their work and sharing their emotions without shame. It was an incredible call for me to be able to stand in my own love for this work, to share my emotions and passion!

- Dutch Canadian Credit Union became the first credit union to become a Certified B Corporation. To date, five credit unions in Canada (representing more than 600,000 members) have become Certified B Corps.
- British Columbia is looking to become the first Commonwealth jurisdiction to introduce benefit corporation legislation.

B Lab United Kingdom, established 2015

- Scotland became the first country to launch a national impact management program.
- More than one hundred large, high-profile (including publicly traded) companies in the UK engaged with the B Corp movement and began to measure their social and environmental performance via the B Impact Assessment.
- B Lab UK delivered its B Leaders training program to create a dynamic group of champions to promote B Corps across the United Kingdom.
- With core funding from the UK Department for International Development, B Lab began a project to map the United Nations Sustainable Development Goals onto the B Impact Assessment.
- The UK government is committed to exploring the creation of a legal form in line with the benefit corporation.

B Lab Taiwan, established 2015

- O-Bank from Taiwan became the first publicly listed B Corp bank in the world.
- At the 2016 B Corp Annual Asia Forum, the president of Taiwan praised B Corporations "for their spirit of innovation and community service" and stressed that the government would continue to support the development of B Corporations and social enterprises.
- At the Taipei Stock Exchange, B Corp certification is recognized as part of initial public offering support documentation.
- The B Corp movement was championed at the Asia-Pacific Economic Cooperation business advisory meeting, getting B Corps on the desk of the leaders of each of APEC's twenty-three member states.

B Lab Europe, established 2015

- Group Danone signed a partnership agreement with B Lab, helping to pave the way for multinationals to measure, compare, and improve their overall social and environmental impact.

WHY WEREN'T WE INVITED? European B Corps pose for a group picture during their summer summit in Cascais, Portugal.

- Geneva, Switzerland, and Calais, France, joined other global cities in running citywide Best For campaigns, which, in partnership with local government and civil society organizations, encourage businesses to measure, compare, and improve their social and environmental impact.

- A coalition of more than two hundred Dutch companies and organizations, including Certified B Corps, appealed to the Dutch government to prioritize the UN Sustainable Development Goals within the upcoming government coalition agreement.

- Following the tireless work of Nativa cofounders Eric Ezechieli and Paolo Di Cesare, Italy became the first country outside of the United States to pass benefit corporation legislation.

B Lab East Africa, established 2017

- B Lab East Africa established partnerships with Sustainable Inclusive Business (part of the largest private sector alliance in Kenya), Self Help Africa, and B Team Africa to promote impact measurement using the B Impact Assessment.

- Enda, the first Kenyan running shoe manufacturer, registered as a benefit corporation in the United States and raised initial funding through B Corp Kickstarter.

- Olivia Muiru, executive director of B Lab East Africa, was recognized as a 2017 Skoll World Forum Emerging Leader.

B Market Builder: Hong Kong, established 2017

- The B Corp idea was presented at the Hong Kong Social Enterprise Summit, at local universities, to the government efficiency unit, and to the undersecretary for home affairs, helping to jumpstart the growth of the B Corp movement in the region.
- Multiple B Leaders courses were conducted in Hong Kong in 2017 with the support of B Lab UK.
- Two Chinese-language books on B Corps were published in Hong Kong in the past two years.

Although we are aware of Shared Value, Conscious Capitalism, and other models, we believe that the B Corp idea is particularly valuable and relevant for Hong Kong. B Corp certification is the only framework that provides a tangible and measurable road map that can help a business make the transition to be a force for good.

K. K. Tse, Education for Good—Hong Kong

B Corp China Team, established 2017

- China's most celebrated and influential economist, Wu Jinglian, publicly recognized benefit corporation legislation and the global B Corp movement as one of the most "notable economic trends," during his keynote speech at the China Europe International Business School CSR [corporate social responsibility] Forum in Beijing, China.

B CORP GROWTH IN CHINA AND HONG KONG. K. K. Tse, founder of B Corp Education for Good, and Robin Lu, COO of First Respond (the first Certified B Corp in China), at an event in Hong Kong.

- The B Generation program, a youth leadership program to inspire, engage, and empower students to lead a global movement of people using business as a force for good, was officially launched at New York University Shanghai, China Europe International Business School, Peking University, and Tsinghua University.
- Professor Chris Marquis at the Harvard Kennedy School published a case study on First Respond, the first Certified B Corp in China. First Respond's achievement as the first B Corp in mainland China was also featured in a national news article in the *China Daily*.

B Lab Korea, established 2018

- The Growth Ladder Fund for start-ups (a program initiated by the Financial Services Committee of Korea) includes "B Corp" as one of the evaluation indicators used to select investments.
- The Korea International Cooperation Agency requires grantees of its Creative Technology Solutions program to obtain B Corp certification.
- The Korean government unveiled its policy road map for social ventures in Korea, indicating support at the government level for the B Corp movement.

DR. JANA'S TIPS: We envision a globally inclusive community of leaders with demographic and socioeconomic representation. The collective impact B Corps could have increases exponentially when we consider cultivating inclusion in a way that allows us to hear directly from the people most affected by the current inequities around the world. We need more diverse B Corp leaders and workforces contributing to and shaping the global dialogue.

Attracting Talent and Engaging Employees

Becoming a Certified B Corporation can help unleash the passion, initiative, and imagination of employees by connecting them with the larger meaning behind their work. Goldman Sachs found that millennials, who currently represent more than 50 percent of the global workforce (and who will represent more than 75 percent of the global workforce by 2025), "have specific needs at work that are dramatically different from previous generations. High among these is a desire to align personal and corporate values. To attract and retain this group, we believe that companies need to provide rewards beyond financial gain."[1]

Research shows that millennials are not just looking for work–life balance, which means having enough time and energy to enjoy life outside of work. They also are looking for work–life integration, which means applying themselves to something that they feel passionate about, so that they can fulfill both an economic need and a need for a higher purpose. Becoming a B Corporation can help you attract, retain, and engage employees around both your company's higher purpose and the B Corp community's collective purpose—to lead a global movement to redefine success in business. Indeed, the *Wall Street Journal* explains that "more companies are touting the B Corp logo, a third-party seal of environmental and social credentials, to attract young job seekers who want an employer committed to both a social mission and the bottom line."[2]

B Corp certification can help you attract top MBA students. In response to student demand, the Columbia, Harvard, New York University, and Yale business schools now offer student loan forgiveness for their MBA graduates who go on to work for Certified B Corporations or benefit corporations. Other academic institutions, like Golden Gate University and Presidio Graduate School, offer tuition discounts to existing employees of Certified B Corporations. Employees of Certified B Corporations also earn a discount when they sign up for LIFT Economy's Next Economy MBA, an online course for entrepreneurs and aspiring entrepreneurs who want to learn key business fundamentals (such as vision, culture, strategy, and operations) from a socially just, environmentally regenerative, and long-term perspective.

DR. JANA'S TIPS: Many B Corps have an opportunity to make a difference in this area. Attracting young, white, liberal, middle-class employees in the United States, for example, is relatively easy for B Corps. Many B Corps in North America struggle to attract racial, ethnic, and socioeconomic diversity. While the B Corp values should and certainly do appeal to marginalized demographics, our sector is not doing enough to facilitate growth in this space. B Corps have a responsibility to do more than post a B Corp logo. Showing up at diverse gatherings, professional associations, and events can build relationships with people outside of our established circles. If we are proactive about diverse recruitment, that inclusive approach will begin to replicate itself and our companies will attract diverse, qualified employees. Passivity will almost always yield homogeneity in recruitment. But diversity in your staff will increase your local and global relevance and your ability to connect with and meet the needs of new and expanding markets.

Increasing Credibility and Building Trust

Ryan remembers the first time he watched Simon Sinek's "How Great Leaders Inspire Action" video. In the video, Sinek explains his theory behind consumer purchasing behavior: "People don't buy what you do; they buy *why* you do it."[3] Sinek says that customers want to connect to the story behind your brand. For example, customers want to know about your purpose in life, why you get out of bed in the morning, and why your organization exists.

In the words of marketing guru Seth Godin, "When price and availability are no longer sufficient advantages (because everything is available and the price is no longer news), then what we are drawn to is the vulnerability and transparency that bring us together, that turn the 'other' into one of us. . . . The people you seek to lead, the people who are helping to define the next thing and the interesting frontier, these people want your humanity, not your discounts."[4]

Patagonia, one of our favorite companies, is a great example of a business that effectively explains the reasoning behind everything it does. Patagonia's mission statement is "Build the best product, cause no unnecessary harm, use business to inspire and implement solutions to the environmental crisis." This mission statement doesn't just describe what the company does (build the best product); it also explains *why* it does it (to use business to inspire and implement solutions to the environmental crisis). Like many, Ryan has a very positive opinion of Patagonia, and he continues to buy its products because its story resonates with him.

A good story, however, is not always the whole story. Consumers increasingly want more than an environmentally friendly product. They want to know what kind of company stands behind a product or service. B Corporation certification can help you build credibility and trust in your brand because it is an independent, rigorous, third-party standard that evaluates every aspect of your business—from how your treat your workers, to your community involvement, to your overall effect on the environment.

This is important because B Corp certification, as opposed to a narrower, more limited evaluation of a building, product, or service, gives a comprehensive snapshot of the whole company, helping to turn the ambiguous concepts of "green" or "responsible" into something concrete and measurable.

As a consulting company with direct influence on many of the major companies in South Africa, we believe we are catalysts for positive change in business and society. B Corp certification demonstrates our credibility to deliver this change.

Stephen Smith, IQbusiness—South Africa

In addition to building consumer trust through rigorous standards, B Corp certification is powerful because it increases transparency and accountability with regard to your company's social and environmental performance. For example, any visitor to the B Corp website can view a B Impact Report, a simple report, similar to the nutritional label on a cereal box, that shows how each Certified B Corporation performed on the Workers, Community, Environment, Governance, and Customers sections of its assessment.[5] This report makes it easy for consumers, investors, policy makers, and the media to tell the difference between good companies and just good marketing.

B Corp is a globally recognized label for companies that have met rigorous standards of performance, accountability, and transparency. The most tangible benefit we have received from B Corp certification is an improvement in the perception of our company's name.

Juliana Arango, Portafolio Verde—Colombia

Research shows that social and environmental credibility is important to the modern consumer. For example, according to Goldman Sachs, consumers identified "being socially responsible" as the factor most likely to influence brand loyalty, compared with lower price, easily available products, quality, and product prestige. Goldman Sachs also reported that 52 percent of U.S. consumers claim that they actively seek information about companies' corporate social responsibility record either "all of the time" or "sometimes." The report concluded, "As more of the millennial generation makes a significant impact on the consumer base, we believe this trend will increase."[6]

DR. JANA'S TIPS: Our goal is a B Corp future where diverse demographics are represented in leadership and within the employee base across our sector worldwide. When people on the fringes of society see themselves reflected in your brand and in our movement, it will generate increased faith in our collective authenticity. In addition, as we diversify the B Corp movement, the issues that plague the world become personal. They become *our* issues because we have expanded our human family to include people different from ourselves. When that happens, real change is inevitable.

Cheryl Pinto,
Ben & Jerry's—USA

Q: Why did you decide to become a B Corp?

A: Using business as a force for good is part of Ben & Jerry's DNA. In a way, we were already a de facto B Corp, because we have a three-part mission and unique governance structure between our parent company, Unilever, and Ben & Jerry's independent board of directors (who really act as "benefit directors"). By joining the community, we navigated new terrain by becoming the first wholly owned subsidiary to certify as a B Corp.

Q: What business benefits do you directly attribute to your B Corp certification?

A: In my role working with Ben & Jerry's supply chain, B Corp certification has provided me with an independent, third-party approach for engaging with our suppliers in a dialogue about our values and advancing our social mission. I require all new key suppliers to take the B Impact Assessment, even if they may not be on track for certification. Sometimes this track has progressed to certification—it's gratifying and energizing to know we've been instrumental in expanding our B Corp community.

Q: If you could change one thing about the B Corp movement, what would it be?

A: It would be powerful to harness and focus the activism energy within the B Corp movement, leveraging the whole community to take a stand on key issues. Our voice needs to be inclusive, clear, and loud.

Benchmarking and Improving Performance

Many B Corps report that one of the biggest benefits of the certification process is the B Impact Assessment, a free tool that measures the social and environmental performance of the entire company on a scale of zero to 200 points. This enables any business to measure the impact of its operations on its workers, its community, and the environment; to compare itself to its industry peers; and to measurably improve its performance over time. The B Impact Assessment is particularly valuable because no matter how sustainable your business already is (or is not), you will undoubtedly find blind spots that you can address to further benefit your stakeholders.

> With B Corp certification, you can look at your score versus other companies and say, "Why didn't we get those points?!" It really helps to get the competitive juices flowing to create more positive impact.

> Steve Beauchesne, Beau's All Natural Brewing—Canada

Patagonia is a great example of a company that uses the B Impact Assessment for continuous improvement. On its initial B Corp certification, in 2012, Patagonia—one of the most eco-friendly companies on the planet—scored 107 out of 200 points. By closely evaluating their results and identifying areas for improvement, Patagonia was able to increase its score to 152 points by 2016. This put them in the 98th percentile, among the highest-scoring B Corps in the world.

The B Impact Assessment is designed to be tough. Rather than trying to get a perfect score on the first try (which is virtually impossible, because no company is perfect), you can use the assessment to measure your company's social and environmental performance, gain valuable insights that can help spark new ideas, and motivate your company to reach for an improved score over time.

Some B Corps, such as Badger Balm, Bancolombia, Ben & Jerry's, and King Arthur Flour are going further by using the B Impact Assessment to benchmark their key suppliers. The assessment's comprehensive, rigorous, and comparable metrics help these companies better understand both the overall impact of their supply chains and the individual performance of their vendors.

In addition, many B Corps use the B Impact Assessment as a guide for their corporate social responsibility reporting. In many cases, substituting the assessment for conventional corporate social responsibility reporting can save considerable time and money.

Protecting a Company's Mission for the Long Term

One of the primary challenges that the B Corp was created to address is raising capital and growing (or selling) a business without diluting the company's original social and environmental values. Certified B Corporations, in addition to meeting rigorous standards of social and environmental performance, amend their governing documents—the legal DNA of their business—to be more supportive of maintaining their social and environmental mission over time.

WHOLE FOODS MARKET. Jay Coen Gilbert, cofounder of B Lab, speaks with John Mackey, CEO of Whole Foods Market, about activist shareholders and the eventual sale of Whole Foods to Amazon.

This expanded legal protection for a company's mission is particularly relevant in succession planning. For example, many businesses, such as Ben & Jerry's, Burt's Bees, and Tom's of Maine, started out with charismatic, dynamic leaders who had strong social and environmental values. However, if the original founders retire, the company wants to take on new investors in order to grow, or the company is put up for sale, those strong core values could be diluted by the new CEO, investors, or owners in favor of increased short-term profits.

By becoming a B Corporation, entrepreneurs can protect their mission by elevating their company's core social and environmental values to the status of law, meaning that new investors and a new board would be obligated to consider both shareholders *and* stakeholders when making decisions in the future. This helps ensure that such a company will continue to benefit society and the environment for the long term.

Patagonia is not a public company and therefore not subject to the risk of an activist hedge fund buying a large stake in the company to try to maximize returns for shareholders. However, Yvon and Malinda Chouinard, the cofounders of Patagonia, are nearing retirement. Yvon and Malinda credit the benefit corporation—which they officially put in place when they registered Patagonia as California's first benefit corporation—with giving them the peace of mind that the environmental mission at the heart of the company's decades-long success would be safe after their retirement.

Patagonia is trying to build a company that could last one hundred years. Benefit corporation legislation creates the legal framework to enable mission-driven companies like Patagonia to stay mission driven through succession, capital raises, and even changes in ownership, by institutionalizing the values, culture, processes, and high standards put in place by founding entrepreneurs.

Yvon Chouinard, Patagonia—USA

Example: Whole Foods Market

Whole Foods Market's sale to Amazon in 2017 is a noteworthy example of the pressure mission-driven founders can face to maximize profits for shareholders. Whole Foods Market was one of the primary drivers of U.S. consumer interest in organic, healthy, and natural foods. Over the past five to ten years, however, many competitors have entered the organic food space, which began to put pressure on Whole Foods's margins. Whole Foods suffered from six consecutive quarters of dropping same-store sales between 2016 and 2017.

Activist investors were quick to take advantage of Whole Foods's tumbling stock price. In 2017, an activist hedge fund purchased a large equity stake in the company, began trying to influence the board of directors, and started to advocate for selling the company. CEO John Mackey was able to orchestrate a sale to Amazon—perhaps the best of several sale scenarios. This experience left Mackey and the Whole Foods team shaken and frustrated.

In an interview with Jay Coen Gilbert, cofounder of B Lab, after the sale, Mackey said he would have liked to have been a test case to see whether the benefit corporation legal structure could have protected Whole Foods Market in a showdown with activist investors: "I always thought B Corps were a good idea . . . but I really didn't think it was necessary. You know, you have this stakeholder model, you take care of your stakeholders, what do you need this legal form for? . . . We had activists come into our stock. . . . They wanted to take over our company; they wanted to force us into a sale. . . . Boy oh boy oh boy, did I wish we were a B Corp. . . . I would have loved to have tested the idea of shareholder activists versus the legal form of a B Corp."

John Mackey expressed his concerns that short-termism is a threat to more than just individual companies like Whole Foods and other "conscious capitalists."

> I know the part of capitalism that is the most diseased. It's the financial sector. It's almost lost its gyroscope of values; it has become just about money and profits.

> When we had shareholder activists, that was really hammered home for me. None of the other values of Whole Foods Market mattered, just how could [they] get a few more dollars out of that stock price? And do whatever it takes to get that. Destroy the company—at 90,000 jobs, $16 billion in sales? "Who cares. If we can make a couple hundred million dollars, throw it all away." That's a very sick part of capitalism.

> I think B Corps and benefit corporations are a tip of a reform movement that capitalism needs as a whole.[7]

DR. JANA'S TIPS: Securing buy-in for inclusive priorities can be challenging. Due to the legal requirement, however, B Corps are uniquely positioned to embed inclusive values and practices into their DNA for the long haul. This is why it's important to be as explicit as possible in naming the impact, vision, mission, and values for your B Corp—and not to omit the DEI aspects. Even if the DEI components of your vision feel far-fetched, out of reach, or heavy-handed, include them anyway. As long as they are stated, we can keep them in view. Ask yourselves hard questions. What does our vision look like if it is wholly inclusive and equitable? Who are we leaving out? How could this better serve our various stakeholders? Seeing through the DEI lens is about keeping your sights set on the desired inclusive outcomes. Stating DEI goals for all to see is a powerful step toward actualization. Perhaps the current team won't need reminding, but the growing team might.

Generating Press and Awareness

Many movements—from cleantech, to microfinance, to buy local, to the co-op movement—are manifestations of the same idea: how to use business for good. The B Corporation amplifies the voice of this diverse marketplace through the power of a credible unifying brand that stands for a better way to do business. In addition, using the power of business to solve social and environmental problems is a positive, innovative, and compelling story that has generated, and continues to generate, a high level of media interest. B Corporations have been featured in thousands of articles in media outlets such as the *Atlantic*, *Conscious Company*, the *Economist*, the *Guardian*, the *New York Times*, and the *Wall Street Journal*. *Fast Company* called the B Corp movement, along with the iPhone and the Human Genome Project, one of "20 Moments from the Past 20 Years that Moved the Whole World Forward."[8]

B Corporations have also been featured on *CBS Evening News*, CNN, and *PBS NewsHour*. For example, Danone CEO Emmanuel Faber spoke on CNBC about the importance of the B Corp movement and Danone North America's decision to certify as a B Corporation. Similarly, in an interview on CNBC, Art Peck, CEO of Gap Inc., spoke about Athleta's decision to become a Certified B Corp and to incorporate as a Delaware public benefit corporation: "[B Corp certification] is a values issue that our customers are super responsive to. The engagement in that brand [Athleta] is amazing, and that's what consumers are looking for today. I don't care if it's a millennial or a seventy-year-old woman. She sees Athleta's B Corp status as something she can relate to from a values standpoint, and it's a really powerful equation."[9]

Storytelling is a key component of transforming the culture and expectations of business. B the Change is the digital storytelling platform for the B Corp movement. B the Change is a collaboration between B Lab, the community of Certified B Corps, and the movement of people using business as a force for good. The publication launched on *Medium* in spring 2017, and in the first year it gathered fourteen thousand followers, all seeking the best practices and lessons shared by the community of B Corps. The articles on B the Change tell the stories of Certified B Corps, benefit corporations, impact-rated funds, and the people, foundations, and organizations committed to growing a new sector of the economy.[10]

Beyond its B the Change storytelling platform on *Medium*, B Lab has helped drive awareness and recognition of the B Corp movement by publishing an annual Best for the World list, which recognizes those companies that score in the top 10 percent of all B Corps worldwide for positive social and environmental impact. Lists include top performers overall as well as for each impact area (Workers, Community, Environment, Customers, and Governance). In 2017, B Lab added a Best for the World: Changemakers list, recognizing companies that had achieved significant improvement year over year. The Best for the World list has received a significant amount of attention from media outlets such as *Bloomberg Businessweek*, *Conscious Company*, *Fast Company*, *Forbes*, the *Guardian*, *Inc.*, and many others.

B Lab partnered with B Corp investment bank Big Path Capital and B Corp media company Real Leaders to promote an annual list of high-growth, high-impact companies, called the Real Leaders 100. B Lab also nominates and acts as an advocate for B Corps to receive top honors, such as a listing among *Bloomberg Businessweek*'s Top Social Entrepreneurs, recognition from the GOOD Company Project, or inclusion in *Inc.* magazine's 500/5,000 List, an annual list of the fastest-growing private companies in the United States.

Finally, more than fifty B Corp champions—such as Rose Marcario from Patagonia, Kat Taylor from Beneficial State Bank, and Aaron Fairchild from Green Canopy—are featured on *Next Economy Now*, a weekly podcast from LIFT Economy.[11] *Next Economy Now* highlights the leaders that are taking a regenerative, bioregional, democratic, diverse, and whole-systems approach to using business as a force for good.

Eloisa Silva,
Mercado Birus—Chile

Q: Why did you decide to become a B Corp?

A: We have been a B Corp since the beginning. We were born as a B Corp to create commercial opportunities for B Corps. We believe that our marketplace would make a difference for people and planet if companies like B Corps were more successful.

Q: What business benefits do you directly attribute to your B Corp certification?

A: We sell products for a wide variety of B Corps. The companies that sell on our platform have told us that it is difficult to communicate their impact through their various sales channels. On Mercado Birus, all B Corps that sell products can communicate how they and their product are different.

Q: What advice do you have for a business that is considering B Corp certification?

A: There is a big difference between saying you want to do business in a different way and being certified by a third party that can verify your claims. Also, I wouldn't think about B Corp certification only in terms of what you can get from the movement. I believe this is about showing you, your partners, and your stakeholders that you are serious about using business as a force for good.

Q: How is your company helping to build a more inclusive economy?

A: We are proud that more than half of the companies who sell their products through our website, www.mercadobirus.com, are businesses founded and/or led by women.

DR. JANA'S TIPS: Our global relevance will expand, as will the press we receive, when we increase diversity within our own companies and within the B Corp movement more broadly. B Corps will be more accessible, relatable, and effective as we meet the needs of a larger group of global citizens.

3

The B Impact Assessment

How to Use Business as a Force for Good

The B Impact Assessment is a comprehensive tool that helps turn the idea of using business as a force for good into a series of concrete, measurable, actionable steps. Whether you want to become a Certified B Corporation or are unsure about B Corp certification but want a free tool to assess, compare, and improve your social and environmental performance, the B Impact Assessment is your starting point.

What Is the B Impact Assessment?

The B Impact Assessment is a free, confidential, easy-to-use online management tool that assesses your company's social and environmental performance on a 200-point scale, compares your results to thousands of businesses, and gives you access to resources and best practice guides that can help you improve your performance over time.[1]

The B Impact Assessment is designed to accommodate all types of businesses, including manufacturers, retailers, agriculture and service companies; businesses of varying size and structure, from sole proprietorships to multinational corporations; and companies from both developed and emerging markets. The B Impact Assessment is flexible, adaptable, and standardized to create an even playing field among all groups. This gives any company the ability to identify where it is doing well and where it has room for improvement, whether the company is just starting out or is taking its thousandth step on this path.

How Much Does the B Impact Assessment Cost?

The B Impact Assessment, including access to the best practice guides, comparative data, and an individualized improvement report, is a free public service provided by B Lab. If you are interested in becoming a Certified B Corporation, there is an annual B Corp certification fee based on your company's annual revenues.[2] Taking the B Impact Assessment does not obligate your company to become a Certified B Corporation.

Will My Data Be Confidential?

Everything you enter into the B Impact Assessment is entirely confidential. None of your company's individual answers will be shared with anyone. In order to create useful comparable metrics for benchmarking purposes, B Lab collects anonymous data from the thousands of users of the B Impact Assessment. This data is only used in aggregate and is not linked to any company's specific answers.

How Much Time Does it Take?

It takes two to three hours to finish a draft of the B Impact Assessment. The most effective strategy for first-timers taking the B Impact Assessment is to keep moving. Make ballpark estimates, skip questions you don't know the answers to, and try to complete the entire assessment relatively quickly. The initial goal is to get a broad overview of the types of questions asked on the B Impact Assessment, not to attempt to answer all of the questions correctly on the first go.

> *I recommend using the BIA [B Impact Assessment] even if you don't decide to certify. Use it to measure what matters—your people, your impact, and your possibilities. You'll be surprised. Before you know it, you will find yourself smiling and wondering why you didn't do this sooner.*
>
> Matt Hocking, Leap—United Kingdom

Who in Our Company Should Complete the Assessment?

For smaller companies, we recommend that the CEO undertake the first round of the B Impact Assessment, because the CEO has a unique perspective on the entire company's operations, knows the strategic direction of the company, and has the power to keep the process moving internally. For larger companies (or for companies where it is not possible to have the CEO involved from the start), we recommend appointing an "internal champion" who is tasked with completing a first draft of the assessment and convening a supporting team to review the results. The internal champion can be anyone—the CFO or COO, your sustainability director or human resources manager, an associate, or even an intern.

What Is a Good Score and What Does My Score Mean?

Any positive score indicates that the company is doing something beneficial for society and the environment. Most companies score somewhere between 40 and 60 points out of a possible 200. Companies interested in becoming a Certified B

Corporation are required to score 80 points or higher. The median score for all Certified B Corps is 95.

What Is the B Impact Report?

The B Impact Report is a free, one-page report that shows how your company performed on the Workers, Community, Environment, Governance, and Customers sections of the B Impact Assessment. This report can help you create a plan to improve your performance in the impact areas that matter most to you.

How Does This Book Differ from the Online Version of the B Impact Assessment?

You will notice that the names, order, and framing of the following sections are similar to but do not exactly mimic the online version of the B Impact Assessment. In addition, not all of the questions that appear in the online version of the assessment are contained in this book. Our goal is to help you better understand the process of taking the B Impact Assessment, to help you address some of the more difficult questions, and to give you best practice ideas on how to improve your score, not to recreate the entire assessment in paper form. The benefit of this approach is that it will make this book applicable to a wider variety of businesses and will help keep the book relevant as B Lab continues to update the B Impact Assessment over time.

How Can I Get More Help?

There are a number of ways to get help on the B Impact Assessment. Try using the Explain This and the Show Example buttons above many of the questions in the assessment, which provide definitions and tips to help you answer each question accurately.

Should I Hire a Consultant?

Many companies prefer to have an external guide to hold them accountable and to help them with tips, best practice ideas, and advice on completing the B Impact Assessment and/or the B Corp certification process. There is a growing community of B Corp consultants who can help your business navigate this process.

A B Impact Team can be another option. B Impact Teams are self-organized groups of college/university students that assist businesses to measure and manage their impact. These student-led consulting teams serve their local communities by using the B Impact Assessment to assess a company's social and environmental performance. Schools around the country have formed B Impact Teams on their campuses to serve local businesses. Reach out to B Lab for recommendations about B Corp consultants and/or B Impact Teams in your local area.

Any Other Advice Before I Start?

Remember, there is no single correct way to be a good company. You will need to choose your own path based on your core values, team interests, industry, and overall business strategy. Use the B Impact Assessment as a framework to reinforce your values, as a road map to help guide your path to achieving your mission, and as a tool to help you implement new socially and environmentally responsible business practices. It is not important where you start, only that you take the next step.

Quick Assessment of Worker Impact

Want to get a quick idea of how good your company is for workers? Take the following thirteen-question Quick Assessment to measure your performance over the past year. You can add up your total at the bottom for a rough idea of how you might score on this section of the B Impact Assessment.

Check the box if you and/or your company . . .

- ☐ share ownership of your company with employees.

- ☐ pay a living wage to employees (including part-time and temporary employees) and independent contractors.

- ☐ have an open-book management process that allows employees to access all available financial and operational data.

- ☐ provide health care for part-time and full-time employees.

- ☐ offer an explicit policy of transgender-inclusive health-care coverage.

- ☐ offer paid caregiver leave.

- ☐ give employees part-time, flextime, or telecommuting options, as appropriate.

- ☐ offer a retirement plan such as a 401(k) or pension and/or profit sharing to all employees.

- ☐ offer a socially responsible investment option in your retirement plan.

- ☐ offer financial products or services that can help meet emergency needs of employees, such as access to free banking services or low-interest loans or by issuing paychecks off schedule as needed.

- ☐ subsidize professional development and training for your workers.

- ☐ have a health and wellness program.

- ☐ conduct regular, anonymous worker satisfaction and engagement surveys.

_____ **Total**

Give yourself one point for each affirmative response.

If you scored from zero to 3, you will have some work do to earn B Corp certification. Alternatively, you can make up ground with an outstanding performance in the other areas.

If you scored from 4 to 6, you are a good candidate for B Corp certification, assuming you perform similarly well on the other sections.

If you scored from 7 to 13, fantastic work! You are likely well on your way to getting the score you need for B Corp certification.

Workers

Being good for workers will mean different things to different people, depending on the size of your company, your industry, and your geographic location. However, many of the underlying themes are applicable to any business. For example, the benefits provided by a solar company may be different from the benefits provided by a bank, but the importance of supporting your employees is equally important in both industries.

In this section, we will highlight some of the ways you can be good for workers, discuss why these are important, explain why they are rewarded on the assessment, and offer tips, resources, and advice to help you make improvements at your company. If you have not already done so, we encourage you to spend a few minutes on the Quick Assessment at the beginning of this section to help you identify areas for improvement.

✓ **Share ownership of your company with employees.**

Why Is This Practice Rewarded?

Your company's ownership structure can be a powerful vehicle to drive impact and inclusion and can offer unique benefits to your business. When it comes to utilizing your business as a force for good, employee ownership is fantastic step in the right direction. Optimizing how your company's success can be shared broadly and address traditional inequalities creates a virtuous cycle of financial success and broader social impact. There are many options available for sharing ownership, including cooperatives, employee stock ownership plans, stock options, phantom stock, and more.

How Can You Implement This at Your Company?

Here are a few key questions to consider that can help your company identify next steps.

- What is the stage, size, industry, and complexity of your company?
- How will current owners exit (or "cash out") of the business?
- How will the goals of employee-owners align (or not) with those of the current ownership?
- What are the potential business benefits?
- What are the other potential challenges that need to be addressed?

COOPERATIVE HOME CARE ASSOCIATES

Adria Powell, Cooperative Home Care Associates—USA

Q: Why did you decide to become a B Corp?

A: The principles and values of being a B Corp were much aligned with the mission and core values of CHCA, particularly as a result of our culture of ownership. As a worker-owned cooperative, we work to integrate the seven principles of cooperatives, many of which match up with the philosophy and essence of being a B Corp.

Q: What was your biggest surprise about becoming a B Corp?

A: To be totally honest, the biggest surprise was having the cofounders of B Lab visit our organization and not only ask us to certify but welcome us, so generously, into the movement. It was complete gratification that we were being recognized as a true business, because we generally don't get that in our industry.

Q: What is your company doing to help build a more inclusive economy?

A: CHCA being in business (and staying in business) is building a more inclusive economy! We bring good jobs to marginalized communities and deliver quality home care services to the most vulnerable and underserved communities. The home care industry is steeped in historical racism and sexism. Through our existence and our culture of worker ownership we give a powerful voice to those who have not been included for generations.

✓ **Pay a living wage to employees (including part-time and temporary employees) and independent contractors.**

Why Is This Practice Rewarded?

Many employers understand that the minimum wage is insufficient to meet many of their employees' basic needs, such as food, housing, child care, and medical care. As a result, employers are starting to pay a "living wage," not only to attract and retain talent but also to help their workers climb out of cyclical poverty. The B Impact Assessment rewards the proactive efforts of employers who implement this practice for their entire workforce.

Perhaps counterintuitively, paying your employees more (that is, at least a living wage) can provide unexpected benefits. For example, Goldman Sachs found that "there is a high correlation across all sectors in terms of cash flow generated relative to payroll per employee." The report goes on to say that this finding "breaks with the common preconception of improving operational efficiency through cutting payroll and, on the contrary, seems to suggest that companies that invest in their workforce will reap exponential benefits."[3]

> *We became a B Corp because we wanted to separate our company from the majority of apparel manufacturers who do not pay fair wages or give employees a dignified working environment.*

> Francisca Caballero, Bordechi—Chile

How Can You Implement This at Your Company?

First, find out what the living wage is for your community (the wage a full-time employee would need to support a family and meet the family's basic needs). The MIT Living Wage Calculator, the Living Wage for Families Campaign, and the

Example: Our Table Cooperative

Our Table, located outside of Portland, Oregon, is a cooperative of people working together to create a resilient and interdependent local food culture. Our Table is one of the only multi-stakeholder cooperatives in the United States. As the name implies, a multi-stakeholder co-op is owned and governed by two or more stakeholder groups. For example, at Our Table:

- worker members raise crops on the fifty-eight-acre certified organic farm and perform aggregation, value-added processing, distribution, and retail services;

- independent producer members, such as regional farmers and food artisans that sell their products through Our Table, help the co-op scale in both product diversity and volume; and

- consumer members, who purchase Our Table's products and subscribe to their offerings, financially support the organization and help foster a transparent, just, and lasting food community.

Our Table models a complete, vertically integrated, community-scale food system. Everyone has a seat at the table, everyone gets a vote, and everyone shares in the profits.

Living Wage Foundation are useful resources for companies based in the United States, Canada, and the United Kingdom, respectively. The Global Living Wage Coalition has resources for companies looking for living wage information for a wide variety of developing countries.[4] If no living wage resource or calculation is available for your location, consider partnering with other businesses or organizations in your area to help have one calculated.

If possible, try to compare your compensation rate to other businesses in your industry. Check your local trade association to see whether it has published a compensation study that you can reference. You also can check the U.S. Bureau of Labor Statistics for wage averages in a variety of industries.

Next, you will want to calculate what percentage of your employees already earns this wage (or higher). Many employers are surprised to find that most of their employees already earn above this minimum threshold. Your wages may need to be adjusted for a much smaller percentage of your workforce than you originally anticipated. You can then calculate what it will cost to raise those employees to a living wage. Remember to factor in potential savings from decreasing attrition and turnover. If there are major financial implications for your business, you may

Worker Ownership: Q&A with Blake Jones of Namaste Solar

Q: Why did you decide to become a worker-owned cooperative?

A: We undertook the transition to a worker-owned cooperative for many reasons, mainly to better align our capital structure with our governance structure. The worker co-op model more closely matches our democratic ideals and more equitably distributes the risk/reward equation of our employee-owners. In addition, this enables us to accept external investors without sacrificing internal control.

Q: Was it difficult to raise capital as a worker-owned cooperative?

A: No. We have had a lot of success raising investment capital. For example, Namaste Solar has raised about $4 million from 120 investors over the last few years. These are highly values-aligned impact investors who are keenly interested in supporting the way we do business. We've all been reading the reports about how the impact investing sector is growing, but Namaste Solar is also seeing it firsthand as we interview investors who are looking for opportunities and companies like ours to invest in. Ultimately, we expect to raise money every few years to provide ongoing growth capital and liquidity for employee-owners and investors who are ready to redeem or divest. We have created a revolving door of employee-owners and values-aligned investors who commit their capital to our cooperative and mission.

---

need to phase in your wage adjustments and/or determine other funding sources to offset costs.

Bring all current employees up to a living wage. To ensure fairness, additional adjustments might be considered for employees who were already making more than a living wage. You will also want to establish a system to ensure that this practice applies to new hires. The living wage changes from year to year based on changes to the cost of living in your area, so best practice is to revisit calculations each year. The last step is to communicate the results of the effort and the expected timeline for adjustments across the company. Staff will want to know about your efforts and how you plan to continue this process over the longer term.

Example: New Belgium Brewing Company

New Belgium Brewing Company has an open-book management program that encourages fiscal transparency, communication, and innovation. For example:

- all new hires learn basic financial concepts and tools during orientation;

- managers share department finances with their teams on a routine basis;

- monthly all-staff sessions are convened to discuss business performance and to enable employees to ask questions;

- remote employees participate in online forums to engage with decision makers and learn about the latest business trends; and

- employees access a variety of information from the company intranet, which provides financials, dashboard metrics with progress updates, and a means to interact with other employees and managers.

New Belgium's open-book management fosters employee engagement and creativity, which in turn drive the company's sustainability efforts. For example, two New Belgium employees recently proposed eliminating twelve-bottle pack dividers, which saved the company more than $280,000, reduced paper waste by 150 tons, and reduced machine downtime.

Anne C. Broughton and Jessica Thomas, *Embracing Open-Book Management to Fuel Employee Engagement and Corporate Sustainability* (Chapel Hill, NC: UNC Kenan–Flagler Business School, 2012).

DR. JANA'S TIPS: Paying a living wage allows everyone, especially entry-level employees, to meet their basic needs. Far too many workers are forced to work multiple jobs—often at the expense of their families. Providing a consistent living wage, combined with fair and objective hiring practices, increases organizational diversity and equity.

✓ Share financial information (for instance, profit and loss statements, balance sheets, and cash flow reports) with your employees. Consider adopting an open-book management process that allows employees to access all available financial and operational data.

Why Is This Practice Rewarded?

Transparency builds trust. Trust is the foundation of strong relationships. Sharing financial information with your employees can range from transparency about basic revenue figures to disclosure of all available financial information (profit and loss statements, balance sheets, and/or salary information). Sharing finances may include, for example, distribution of information directly to employees or simply sharing information during a presentation.

In addition, some companies have an open-book management process that enables employees to access real-time financial and operational data. An open-book program can contribute to the overall success of the company by empowering employees and departments to set and maintain their own financial goals. For more information on open-book management, check out the book *The Great Game of Business* by Jack Stack and Bo Burlingham.

How Can You Implement This at Your Company?

The factors that contribute to this decision will be different for every company. If you currently do not share any financial information, we would suggest sharing with your employees at least basic financial figures, such as core revenue sources and operational costs, on a regular basis.

In addition to sharing information, it can be mutually beneficial to teach employees why certain financial and operational data is valuable. For example, if you make a product, consider sharing trends, such as which product lines are growing in revenue or margin. Explain the underlying assumptions of your financial projections. You also should be transparent about unresolved challenges (for example, "We see an opportunity to reduce costs on our new product line, but we are not sure about our next steps"). This is an opportunity to motivate and engage your employees by helping them learn about new areas of the business.

DR. JANA'S TIPS: When considering increased financial transparency, a common concern we hear is about sharing information related to compensation. This information is often treated as private and confidential. However, the decision to keep certain information private should be balanced with the reality that there are pervasive disparities in compensation among genders, ethnicities, ages, and nationalities. Sharing compensation details can help leadership remain fair and equitable in their allocation of salaries and other resources. Financial transparency can support more objective compensation practices that ultimately help employees feel more respected and included.

Our main challenge with sharing financial data was engaging employees with nonbusiness backgrounds. What we had to do was (1) include business/financial basics during employee orientations, (2) simplify indicators to be as straightforward as possible, (3) assign team heads to be the owner for internal education, (4) empower colleagues to actively propose what to include in their team statistics, and (5) keep improving and improving.

Harris Cheng, Greenvines—Taiwan

✓ **Provide health care for part-time and full-time employees. Include a transgender-inclusive health-care policy.**

Why Is This Practice Rewarded?

Providing health-care benefits to employees gives them access to affordable, quality health care even if they have other obligations (such as family care or education) that prevent them from working full time. Additionally, employees who have access to health care are more likely to stay healthy, making them less likely to miss work or come to work sick.

Transgender people access health care for all the same reasons that anyone else does, but sometimes their transgender status is regarded by insurance carriers (and some care providers) as a barrier to care. Businesses, as consumers of group health insurance products, can advocate on behalf of the transgender people insured on their group health insurance plans. Employers should work with their insurance carriers or administrators to remove transgender exclusions and to provide comprehensive transgender-inclusive insurance coverage.

How Can You Implement This at Your Company?

If you operate in the United States or another country where health insurance is commonly provided by employers, try using health risk questionnaires and focus groups to identify the best health benefits for your unique team. This will enable you to work with health providers to tailor benefits to best serve your unique workforce.

To determine whether your health insurance plan (or prospective plan) is transgender inclusive, the Human Rights Campaign recommends that you examine your plan's exclusions, confirm the availability of transgender-related services, contact your benefits manager for any clarification needed, and obtain an affirmative answer from your insurance administrator that your plan covers the health-care needs of transgender individuals without exclusion.[5]

✓ **Provide paid caregiver leave to your workers.**

Why Is This Practice Rewarded?

Family-friendly business practices like paid caregiver leave make it easier for employees to integrate work with time spent building healthy families. Paid caregiver leave will benefit your employees regardless of gender. Paid caregiver leave has been demonstrated to increase employee retention and engagement (especially among women), to minimize the costs of training new employees, and to increase the diversity of the workforce.

Many companies have shifted away from the term "maternity" leave to the gender-neutral "primary caregiver" leave. Although this shift is well-intentioned, some commentators argue that this is still makes paid leave contingent on an employee identifying as the "primary caregiver." Authors

Example: Change.org

All new parents at Change.org, biological or adoptive, are eligible for eighteen weeks' fully paid leave during their first year with the child. Details are coordinated with a supervisor and human resources staff to accommodate everyone's needs. This policy communicates to employees that Change.org values parents and understands the importance of family to a healthy workplace.

No Margin, No Mission

It is important to note that paid caregiver leave, especially in places like the United States, where it is not fully covered by the government, can be challenging for businesses to implement—even if the leadership of a company is deeply aligned with the need for and value of such a policy. For example, when reviewing this book before publication, Mike Hannigan, president of Give Something Back Office Supplies (a founding B Corp based in Oakland, California), wrote:

> There is no doubt that paid caregiver leave is incredibly important and should be rewarded on the B Impact Assessment. With that being said, I believe there should be some acknowledgment that policies like this are not only a matter of ethics or values. Despite the undeniable pluses like retention, productivity, and morale, decisions like these are directly linked to the financial profile of the enterprise. Readers may be frustrated if policies like this are presented in a manner that is disconnected from the financial and operational realities of running a business. Change.org may be able to hold out when key employees are off for eighteen weeks and still satisfy their customers. It would be very difficult for us.

Mike brings up a great point. Becoming a Certified B Corp does not mean you have to make every possible social and environmental improvement without regard to your bottom line. A common phrase in social entrepreneurship circles is "No margin, no mission." You have to run a financially sound business in order to create a positive impact. This is why we believe that the B Impact Assessment process is valuable. It is not about being perfect from the start. It is about seeing where your company is at, identifying what is possible, and striving for continuous improvement.

Hilary Rau and Joan C. Williams, in the *Harvard Business Review*, write, "Primary-caregiver policies are holdovers from the days when maternity leave was available to birth mothers only, with partners and adoptive parents left out in the cold. Such policies reflect the assumption that families will have one primary caregiver, supported by a partner with few, or no, caregiving responsibilities. It's the old-fashioned homemaker/breadwinner model clothed in a tissue-thin veneer of gender neutrality."[6]

Rau and Williams argue that companies need only two categories for parental leave: disability leave for women who are physically unable to work due to pregnancy, childbirth, or related conditions, and parental leave that's equally available to all employees, regardless of gender or caregiver status. Rau and Williams urge companies to consider that "paid leave is a powerful tool for recruiting and retaining top talent—*if* it sends a strong signal that a company values its employees and is committed to equity and diversity in the workplace. Employers can avoid undercutting this powerful message by making sure that their paid leave policy applies equally to *all* new parents—mothers and fathers, biological and adoptive, LGBT, salaried and hourly—without requiring that employees first prove themselves to be primary caregivers" (authors' emphasis).

How Can You Implement This at Your Company?

If you are interested in moving forward with a parental leave policy, here are some basic steps to help you implement this practice at your company.

- Calculate the potential cost of paid parental leave. Balance this against the reputational benefits, competitive edge in recruitment, and increased employee productivity and retention.

- Create a protocol to help manage the transition to leave. For example, a few months before an employee goes on caregiver leave, ask them to bring a list of all the projects they are working on and who they think might be suitable to handle them while they are gone. Reassure the employee that if no one comes to mind, the company will figure someone out and/ or hire extra help. Outline a transition plan based on conversations with the employee.

- Create a protocol to help returning employees get back to work more smoothly. When the leave-taker returns, his or her supervisor should hold a meeting to discuss the plan, which should include check-ins during the ramp-up period to ensure that the returning employee is getting enough work, and appropriate work.

- Creating the right workload balance. Some caregivers get too little work when they return from leave, others get too much. One example is to provide all returning leave-takers with a 50 percent schedule that gradually builds back to full time (defined by their target schedule).

- Draft a formal policy to provide clarity and consistency for your staff. Communicate the policy to employees. If needed, continue to iterate and tweak the policy to make it better over time.

DR. JANA'S TIPS: Paid caregiver leave is among the benefits that help people through challenging life stages. These life stages can be particularly significant setbacks for marginalized demographics, who may not have access to savings, family assistance, liquid assets, or supplemental insurance to support such events. Inclusive policies, like those mentioned above, create space for people to live their lives and still receive support. Whether people need to care for their new children or their aging parents, this benefit supports inclusion and can increase employee loyalty.

✓ **Give employees part-time, flextime, or telecommuting options, as appropriate.**

Why Is This Practice Rewarded?

Many businesses report that the recruitment and retention of skilled workers is one of the most important challenges they face. Workplace flexibility—giving people more control over their work time and schedules—has been shown to improve employee engagement, increase job satisfaction, and reduce stress. Workplace flexibility, because it aids recruitment and increases employee retention and engagement, is also better for the bottom line.

How Can You Implement This at Your Company?

A successful flexible work program requires clear organizational policies and guidelines. It requires managers to be knowledgeable about policies and to promote flexibility. It also requires employees to consider, when proposing flexible work strategies, the needs of the job, their coworkers, customers, and the company. A report by Corporate Voices for Working Families recommends a number of steps that businesses can take to get started.

- **Engage employees in developing solutions that meet business and personal needs.** Start with a solid understanding of the business parameters, asking employees what they want, listening to their ideas, and being open to creative new ways of scheduling. Clearly communicate expectations, providing the necessary information and tools, and then empower and trust employees to deliver the required results.

- **Create accountability and provide support for managers.** In companies that have experienced sustained success with flexible work options, executives connect flexibility to their core values, understand the relationship between flexibility and employee engagement, and hold their managers accountable for providing flexibility to their employees.
- **Develop clear policies to ensure consistent, fair treatment.** Clear policies, guidelines, and processes provide a strong framework for managers charged with approving flexibility requests. This is particularly important for managers faced with difficult decisions or competing requests.

The Corporate Voice for Working Families report concludes that "companies that have created successful flexibility options for their lower wage workers receive a high return on their investments because of the many positive impacts on employees and the business: better recruitment and retention of talent, increased engagement, lower levels of stress and burnout, greater productivity and effectiveness, better customer service, and finally more positive financial results."[7]

DR. JANA'S TIPS: Flextime can be the variable that makes or breaks a workplace experience for vulnerable populations—everyone from single parents to blended families to folks with disabilities or who care for people who are differently abled. People with little to no savings, adult college students, and those caring for elderly parents are among the countless populations who benefit from flextime. Allowing the practice will communicate to your team that you value their life apart from their work. If your concern is that people will use flextime to avoid working, know that accountability is important. That said, companies with successful flextime programs, like Patagonia, note that employees who feel valued and trusted to get their work done also tend to be more engaged, loyal, and collaborative.

✓ **Offer a retirement plan such as a 401(k) or pension. In addition, offer a socially responsible investment option for your retirement plan.**

Why Is This Practice Rewarded?

A key component of building a business with loyal, engaged employees is helping them build long-term financial security. Creating an employee retirement plan can be a smart way to attract and retain valuable employees,

EILEEN FISHER

Eileen Fisher,
Eileen Fisher—USA

Q: Why did you decide to become a B Corp?

A: We have been passionately committed to social and environmental responsibility for over three decades. B Corp certification, and the recognition it provides, allows us to take a bold step in sharing who we are and what we believe in, and to make a greater impact in the world as a leader in the fashion industry.

Q: What is your company doing to help build a more inclusive economy?

A: In our benefit corporation charter, we specified that we want to use our company to create an inclusive workplace ("that respects and honors differences in gender, age, race, ethnicity, religion, sexual orientation, and political views") as well as to use our business operations to support the fair treatment of all people.

In our supply chain, we have exciting initiatives exploring how to ensure fair wages and benefits for all workers. As a woman-founded and majority women-owned company, we are also actively looking at all aspects of our business to understand how we can lift up women and create a more gender-equitable world.

Q: What advice do you have for a business that is considering B Corp certification?

A: Certification is what you make of it. It requires time, effort, and resources to obtain initial certification and to go through recertification. However, the opportunity for community partnership, employee engagement, customer education, and greater understanding and guidance around our impact on the world is incredibly beneficial.

If your company does not have a socially responsible fund but already funds a retirement plan, you will still receive credit on the B Impact Assessment. The SRI option is an incremental opportunity to do more good.

DR. JANA'S TIPS: Retirement plans can be valuable tools for all people. This is especially true for historically marginalized populations that have not had access to generational wealth. Retirement plans can help restore economic balance for families and communities that have been subjected to endless cycles of debt and poverty. Retirement plans such as a 401(k), paired with financial education, can be particularly helpful. It is important to assume that not everyone has the same understanding of and access to financial literacy and investment planning.

How Can You Implement This at Your Company?

If your company does not have a plan, setting one up is relatively inexpensive. If you already have a plan, try giving your employees an anonymous survey to see whether an SRI option would be valuable to them. The Society for Human Resource Management found that the number of SRI funds is likely to double in the next few years, to match the rapidly growing interest.[8] Next, ask your benefits administrator whether there are any SRI options available in your plan. If not, consider searching the B Corp website for companies that have expertise in this field.

✓ **Offer financial products or services that can help meet emergency needs of employees. This can include access to free banking services or low-interest loans, issuing paychecks off schedule on an as-needed basis, or other innovative practices.**

Why Is This Practice Rewarded?

Creating access to equitable short-term loans and long-term financial planning can help employees become more financially resilient, especially those who may face barriers to accessing traditional financial services. Supporting employees who are at risk of financial insecurity can increase employee loyalty and reduce turnover.

Example: Rhino Foods

Rhino Foods is an ice cream ingredients manufacturer with roughly 150 employees. As a benefit to employees, Rhino, in partnership with a local credit union, offers a loan of up to $1,000 to all workers in good standing who have been at the company for sixty days or more. Relatively low-interest loans are available without a credit check—applicants' tenure at the company is proof enough of their ability to pay—and the credit union typically distributes cash on the day of application. Loans are paid back via payroll deductions.

For Rhino, the program has been successful. Since beginning the program, Rhino has facilitated hundreds of loans totaling hundreds of thousands of dollars. Business has been strengthened: within three years of implementing the benefit, turnover rates fell from 39 percent to less than 15 percent. The company reports that productivity, attendance, and loyalty have gone up.[9]

How Can You Implement This at Your Company?

Inspired by the B Corp Inclusive Economy Challenge and the model shared by B Corp Rhino Foods, Heather Paulsen Consulting established Helping Employees Access Loans, a collaborative income-advance program that all B Corps in Mendocino County, California, can offer their employees. Paulsen identified a local bank that was willing to take 100 percent of the risk of the HEAL loans. The HEAL program, along with employer-sponsored income-advance programs, offers a viable and affordable alternative to payday loans, providing workers with the financial assistance they need to get through financial emergencies. Programs like HEAL create low-risk opportunities to build credit, offer valuable financial education, and often result in increased savings. Here are some of the steps you can take to provide better financial services for employees:

- Solicit input from your employees to understand their particular financial needs.

- Calculate the potential costs of providing financial services support, being sure to include the potential financial benefits.

- Seek partnerships with local nonprofit organizations, financial institutions, government organizations, or other businesses that could help provide beneficial services.

- Draft a written policy.
- Communicate the policy and timeline to employees. Think carefully about your workforce's language preferences, reading levels, communication channels, and preferred information mediums (such as online communications, written reports, videos, or presentations by peers). This will enable you to craft communications to ensure that your employees clearly understand the value of the new programs.

DR. JANA'S TIPS: There is often a correlation between marginalized or protected demographics and socioeconomic disadvantages like compromised credit, lack of financial literacy, and excessive debt. These challenges can make emergencies even harder to manage. One medical emergency can bankrupt a family that doesn't have access to external support. Emergency financial services can help employees stay on track, regardless of demographic. It is an inclusive practice that communicates how much you value the well-being of employees and their families. Examples like the Helping Employees Access Loans program show that employers do not necessarily need to take on the financial risk of providing these benefits.

✓ **Subsidize professional development and training for your workers.**

Why Is This Practice Rewarded?

In his book *Drive*, author Daniel Pink explains that employees are motivated by three primary drives: autonomy, mastery, and purpose. According to Gallup, 87 percent of millennials say professional development or career growth opportunities are a very important part of their job.[10] Providing employees with educational and/or professional development opportunities helps to challenge them and encourages them to build mastery in a particular domain. It also can help prepare them to move into management or other internal positions.

How Can You Implement This at Your Company?

To learn what type of professional development will fit your company's objectives and needs, talk to your employees about the kinds of training they seek. These could include core job skills, cross-job training, or life skills (such as financial literacy or English as a second language). When deciding what to offer, focus on access to make sure there are no unintended biases or barriers to participation (for instance, caregivers may not be able to attend evening events).

To encourage professional development, some B Corps offer an annual training budget of $1,000 to $2,500 per employee, to be used at the employee's discretion. According to a recent American Society for Training & Development *State of the Industry* report, the average direct expenditure per employee on training and development in the United States is $1,182.[11] A shortcut you can use to calculate a new training budget is to multiply your total annual payroll by 1 to 5 percent. A discretionary training budget allows employees to decide which professional development opportunities they want to pursue, such as industry trade shows, conferences, or trade-specific accreditation.

DR. JANA'S TIPS: Be mindful to offer educational opportunities in an equitable and fair manner. Create objective criteria for determining what the company will and will not pay for. This will help you avoid the appearance of bias. The opportunity for skills development is a significant benefit, used by employees as a path to promotion. So it is essential that the opportunities you create are equitable and inclusive. When planning a training, things to consider include accessibility of physical spaces and materials, languages used, access to or cost of transportation, geographic location and time zone, level of literacy, access to the internet and computers, pay implications for hourly workers, and access to child care. As part of continuous improvement of your programs and policies, make sure you solicit feedback from employees who do not take part in professional development opportunities to learn about any hidden barriers to participation.

✓ **Expand your company's health and wellness programs.**

Why Is This Practice Rewarded?

Typically, wellness programs focus on stress management, mental health, fitness, nutrition, and work–life balance. In addition to benefiting individual workers, employee wellness programs have been shown to benefit a company's bottom line. For example, Johnson & Johnson estimates that its health and wellness program had a return on investment of $2.71 for every dollar spent between 2002 and 2008. A study of a different employer found an even higher return: every dollar invested in healthy interventions yielded $6 in health-care savings.[12]

BluPlanet, a B Corp recycling collection provider based in Calgary, Alberta, offers a diverse curriculum of training courses and programs for employees. Some courses and programs support employee professional development while others are geared toward improving the company's systems. For courses that benefit the employee's personal development but do not have an immediate impact on the firm, the company pays partial tuition, as determined during compensation review. Employees who complete professional development courses may receive additional compensation. The company pays 100 percent for courses and programs directly related to systems improvements.

One innovative way of reducing stress is to keep workers and their families closer together. Patagonia has provided subsidized, on-site child care since 1984. Founder Yvon Chouinard asserts that on-site child care is a profit center rather than a financial burden. "Seventy-one percent of our employees are women, and many occupy high-level management positions," says Chouinard. "Studies have shown that it costs a company an average of fifty thousand dollars to replace an employee—from recruiting costs, training, and loss of productivity. Our child care center helps us retain our skilled moms."[13]

How Can You Implement This at Your Company?

There are many different things you can do to promote employee health and wellness. For example, B Corps offer a variety of benefits to workers, such as gardening classes, office yoga, discounted gym memberships, lunchtime running groups, organic fruit and healthy snacks, juicing classes, free access to a nutritionist, wellness goal setting, or a company-hosted community supported agriculture program.

If you are inspired to create (or improve) your health and wellness program, consider talking to your insurance carrier about possible discounts and incentives. It is in their best interest to offer wellness options. The healthier your employees are, the fewer claims insurers will need to pay. In addition, try putting your health and wellness policy in writing. A formal policy is a useful communication tool that can help support a culture of wellness.

DR. JANA'S TIPS: Workplace culture can affect employee health—and organizational culture can be created by default or by design. Consider creating an organizational culture vision statement. Work with your staff to craft a culture statement that speaks to the experience you want employees to have at your company. Then find ways to reinforce that message so that you can reference it when people conduct themselves in ways that are inconsistent with your cultural vision. A simplified, placeholder statement, one that can be expanded and made more specific, is "A workplace that works well for everyone." This holds that no matter who you are as an employee, whatever your background, you should be able to apply the skills for which you were hired, in a healthy and supportive workplace.

✓ **Conduct regular, anonymous worker satisfaction and engagement surveys.**

Why Is This Practice Rewarded?

How motivated and engaged are your employees? Over the past several years, research has identified a strong link between a company's financial performance and the engagement levels of its employees. For example, a recent Gallup study found that "organizations with engaged employees experience positive business performance, while workplaces with not engaged or actively disengaged employees are more likely to experience lower productivity."[14]

In addition, disengaged employees have been shown to have the same level of health problems as the unemployed, including higher rates of obesity and chronic illnesses. Gallup notes that "the high rates of obesity and chronic illnesses these groups report could have a major effect on their long-term health." This research is especially troubling because 71 percent of American workers report that they are "not engaged" or are "actively disengaged" in their jobs.[15] Companies that regularly track metrics such as job satisfaction, retention, turnover, and diversity will have a better chance of identifying problems before they expand.

DR. JANA'S TIPS: When it comes to diversity, equity, and inclusion, employee feedback is critical. People are often afraid to bring issues to leadership, fearing retribution. It is important to provide employees with periodic anonymous or confidential opportunities to shed light on what is really happening within the organization. If employees do not feel safe during or after the feedback collection process, they will shut down and refrain from sharing in the future. Unfortunately, that's how companies end up on the front page of the news—exposed for messy people problems that could have been solved with honest conversation and targeted intervention. See appendix B for two sample DEI surveys you can use with your staff.

How Can You Implement This at Your Company?

Here are some sample questions you could ask on your employee satisfaction survey:

- How meaningful is your work?
- How challenging is your work?
- In a typical week, how often do you feel stressed at work?
- How well are you paid for the work you do?
- How much do your opinions about work matter to your coworkers?
- How often do the tasks assigned to you by your supervisor help you grow professionally?
- How many opportunities do you have to get promoted where you work?
- How likely are you to look for another job outside the company?

In addition to asking good questions, there are a number of best practices that can help you collect the most useful results.

- **Plan on following up on areas of concern immediately.** It can be very disheartening for an employee to spend time responding to a satisfaction survey, only to have nothing change in response to their input. Try to address employee concerns quickly. Otherwise, employees may feel disenchanted by the survey process.

- **Make gathering names optional.** You want employees to be as honest as possible when they take your survey. Some may feel more interested in providing transparent feedback if including their name with their responses is optional.
- **Use clear language.** Avoid using buzzwords and corporate language that employees may not understand.
- **Avoid tinkering with the words.** Keep the wording constant among surveys and from year to year. This way you can be sure you are measuring the same aspects of your company's culture.

If you are interested in a free employee satisfaction survey (which also includes questions related to the company's social and environmental performance), visit the LIFT Economy website.[16] If you are interested in free samples of diversity, equity, and inclusion surveys, see appendix B of this book. Dr. Jana provides two sample surveys—a leadership structural inclusion survey and an employee organizational DEI survey—so that readers can experience the types of questions they should be asking when considering starting (or restarting) inclusion-focused work.

Quick Assessment of Community Impact

Want to get a quick idea of how good your company is for the community? Take the following fifteen-question Quick Assessment to measure your performance over the past year. You can add up your total at the bottom for a rough idea of how you might score on this section of the B Impact Assessment.

Check the box if you and/or your company . . .

☐ have a diverse group of owners, executives, employees, and board members.

☐ fill open positions with women; people of color; LGBTQ, disabled, or low-income people; or other previously excluded populations.

☐ have specific, measurable diversity improvement goals that are reviewed by senior executives and/or the board of directors.

☐ include in all job postings a statement indicating a commitment to diversity, equity, and inclusion.

☐ conduct a pay equity analysis by gender, race, ethnicity, and/or other demographic factors and, if necessary, implement equal compensation improvement plans or policies.

☐ determine the multiple that your highest-paid worker earns compared to your lowest-paid full-time worker.

☐ create job opportunities for chronically underemployed populations, such as at-risk youth, homeless individuals, or individuals who were formerly incarcerated.

☐ provide your employees with diversity, equity, and inclusion trainings.

☐ have a written community service policy, offer incentives for employees to organize service days and/or volunteer activities, and set goals to increase the percentage of employees who participate.

- [ ] have a formal commitment to donating a percentage of revenue to charity, match charitable contributions made by employees, and/or join a third-party organization that certifies charitable giving, such as 1% for the Planet.

- [ ] purchase from local suppliers or from suppliers owned by women, people of color, or individuals from other underrepresented populations.

- [ ] have a formal, written supplier code of conduct that specifically holds the company's suppliers accountable for social and environmental performance.

- [ ] bank with a Certified B Corporation, a credit union, a community development financial institution, and/or a member of the Global Alliance for Banking on Values.

- [ ] disclose on your website the names of your suppliers (and their social and environmental performance).

- [ ] work within your industry to develop social and environmental standards.

_____ **Total**

Give yourself one point for each affirmative response.

If you scored from zero to 3, you will have some work do to earn B Corp certification. Alternatively, you can make up ground with an outstanding performance in the other areas.

If you scored from 4 to 6, you are a good candidate for B Corp certification, assuming you perform similarly well on the other sections.

If you scored from 7 to 15, fantastic work! You are likely well on your way to getting the score you need for B Corp certification.

Community

The first step to being good for the community is to see your business as connected to the local, national, and global communities in which it resides. Indeed, businesses that behave like socially and environmentally responsible citizens can benefit from an improved ability to attract and retain top talent, generate positive media attention, and increase customer goodwill.

The B Corp community must continually ask itself who we are as a community, who we want to be as a community, and who is missing from our community. When we assess local, national, and global impact, how closely are we tracking with the needs and concerns of the least among us? Who is being overlooked, and what can we do to correct that?

As in the Good for Workers section, this section will highlight some of the practices that are good for the community, discuss why they are important, explain why they are rewarded on the assessment, and offer you tips for implementing these practices in your company.

✓ **Ensure that you have a diverse group of owners, executives, and board members. Fill open positions with women; people of color; LGBTQ, disabled, or low-income people; or other previously excluded populations.**

Why Is This Practice Rewarded?

The benefits of diversity are well documented. McKinsey & Company found that companies with a high representation of female executives have a 47 percent higher average return on equity than do other businesses. Credit Suisse found that companies with one or more female board members have superior share price performance relative to industry peers with all-male boards of directors.[17]

More studies are starting to show that these benefits also apply when working with other diverse groups, such as ethnic minorities, people with disabilities, and lesbian, gay, bisexual, and transgender communities. For example, one study found that employees of gay managers tend to have 35 percent higher job satisfaction and engagement.[18]

Mainstream business leaders are advocating for diversity as well. For example, BlackRock manages more than $6 trillion in assets and is the largest investor in the world. In his 2018 letter to CEOs, Larry Fink, the CEO of BlackRock, said BlackRock "will continue to emphasize the importance of a diverse board. Boards with a diverse mix of genders, ethnicities, career

Sweet Livity

Diana Marie Lee,
Sweet Livity—USA

Q: Why did you decide to become a B Corp?

A: I learned about B Corps back in 2015 from one of my mentors, Ajax Greene. I had been supporting nonprofit social justice leaders in North Carolina and the San Francisco Bay Area to become more entrepreneurial in their approach to serving the community and raising money for the work of their organizations. Those experiences inspired me to learn more about social entrepreneurship and social enterprises.

As I began to learn about the B Corp movement and its focus on a triple bottom line of helping people and the planet, not only profit, I was inspired. Years later, when I left the nonprofit sector, burned out and disillusioned, I went on a healing journey to recover. When I returned to the United States, having reclaimed better health, my joy, and a sense of purpose, I knew I wanted to do my community work as a B Corp.

Q: What was your biggest surprise about becoming a B Corp?

A: I was surprised that there were not more B Corps owned and led by people of color. The B Corp movement seems like it operates in a silo, like a well-kept secret, within a small percentage of the business community. I want to change that. I don't want B Corps to be a hidden secret anymore, especially to those visionary people who need a viable way to support their communities without sacrificing their needs or the needs of their families.

experiences, and ways of thinking have, as a result, a more diverse and aware mind-set. They are less likely to succumb to groupthink or miss new threats to a company's business model. And they are better able to identify opportunities that promote long-term growth."[19]

Despite the wide diversity of religious beliefs, ethnicities, sexual orientations, physical abilities, and genders in society, most of these communities are vastly underrepresented at the senior executive level. For example, women represent approximately 50 percent of the workforce but represent only 17 percent of board seats of companies in the Fortune 1,000.[20] However, thanks to the efforts of many forward-thinking businesses, advocates, and industry associations, diversity at all management levels is starting to rise.

How Can You Implement This at Your Company?

Expanding the diversity of your company is incredibly worthwhile. The following are a few tips to help you on your journey.

- **Start with affirming and articulating your key commitments to inclusion.** An inclusive work culture will be necessary to create a work environment that supports, attracts, and retains a more diverse workforce.

- **Create a baseline by measuring diversity and inclusion in your company.** You may do this by evaluating current diversity data and/or by conducting an inclusion survey. See appendix B of this book for two sample DEI surveys from TMI Consulting.

- **Create specific, measurable diversity improvement goals that are reviewed by senior executives and/or the board of directors.** You may want to take into account the diversity of the overall local population, which you can learn from census data or local population surveys. Consider tying specific diversity goals to each team, recruiter, and hiring manager, then evaluate and reward success through annual performance evaluations.

- **Perform an inclusion audit of your current recruiting processes, website, and job descriptions to determine where the process excludes or ignores underrepresented people.** For example, be conscious of how you draft job descriptions. Research has shown that using certain phrases in job descriptions, such as "rock star," "ninja," or "a proven track record," can result in fewer female applicants. Along the same lines, if a potential applicant reads that you're looking for a "good cultural fit," they might get the impression that your company is only looking to hire people similar to those who are already on the team.[21]

- **Ensure that you include in all job postings a statement indicating a commitment to diversity, equity, and/or inclusion.** For example, here is the language B Lab uses for its own job postings:

> B Lab values a diverse workforce. Women, people of color, people with disabilities, and members of the LGBTQ community are strongly encouraged to apply. B Lab believes an equitable and inclusive work environment and a diverse, empowered team are key to achieving our mission. We're not looking for candidates who are "culture fits." We're looking for candidates who can expand our culture, challenge business as usual, and bring their whole selves to work. We strive to provide those candidates with an equitable and accessible recruitment process. If we can offer accommodations for you in the recruitment process or you have feedback on how to make our recruiting more accessible, please let us know.

- **Create a plan to improve recruiting processes based on your findings.** Intentionally reach out to communities that are unlikely to have heard about your company. For example, create a relationship with schools in your area that have a diverse student body. In the United States, this could mean attending career fairs at places like historically black colleges and universities, tribal colleges and universities, and community colleges.

We've been really proactive about meeting professors and deans in business schools and departments at historically black colleges and universities. We want to make sure that they know that we are interested in their students for full-time jobs and internships/fellowships.

Paige Bagwell, The Redwoods Group—USA

- **When interviewing, use the same questions for every applicant.** This allows you to measure each interviewee against the same criteria and limits biases. For example, Method uses the following behavioral questions for its interviews:

What achievement are you most proud of?

Tell me about a time you have "made things happen" for yourself or your team.

Share the most difficult and complex situation in which you set clear, lofty goals for yourself (and others, if applicable) and then pursued those goals with enthusiasm and energy.

Share an instance that showcased your drive to be satisfied with concrete, stellar results.

How do you handle being wrong? Tell me about a recent situation where you had to admit that you were wrong.

- **Create a committee that is explicitly responsible for diversity, equity, and inclusion at the company.** Work with the committee to identify opportunities for improvement in retaining, promoting, and engaging diverse staff. Alternatively, create and/or hire a diversity manager or chief diversity officer.
- **Regularly survey your team to measure and track both your internal diversity and the inclusivity of your work environment.** Continually update goals as relevant.
- **Reach out to a local B Corp and ask them about their experiences with creating a diverse leadership team and workforce.**

Method has done a lot of work around identifying unconscious biases in its interview process. Unconscious bias refers to a bias that happens automatically, is outside of our control, and is triggered by our brain making quick judgments and assessments of people and situations. Our biases are influenced by our background, cultural environment, and personal experiences. The table on the next page details some of the common mistakes Method has identified and now trains its employees to watch out for during the interview process.

DR. JANA'S TIPS: If your company is like most, diversity is concentrated at the bottom, in the entry-level, lowest-paying positions. Even if you have a few managers or leaders from underrepresented groups, those people are likely the exception. Diversifying the highest levels of your organization is not only proven to be excellent for business but also helps generate, in a virtuous circle, more diversity and inclusion.

Having visible minority leadership supports sustainable structures that demonstrate to other underrepresented people that your organization is inclusive across the board. It gives people something to aspire to by demonstrating that your organization is willing and able to promote diversity. Without such representation, people are apt to believe that they are shut out of leadership opportunities and are therefore less likely to work toward promotion. A lack of visibly diverse leadership perpetuates the self-limiting belief that "I cannot be successful here because no one who looks like me has been." This is why we often see underrepresented employees leaving for other opportunities where they *know* they can be promoted.

✓ **Conduct a pay equity analysis by gender, race, ethnicity, and/or other demographic factors and, if necessary, implement equal compensation improvement plans or policies.**

Why Is This Practice Rewarded?

Employers have a responsibility to pay equally across gender, race, sexual orientation, age, socioeconomic status, and more. Ensuring equal pay for equal work ensures that all employees have the same recognition, rewards, and opportunities for financial well-being. Proactively managing pay equity enables businesses to access a broader and more diverse pool of talent and perspectives, can improve overall employee engagement, and can reduce the risk of legal action.

Common Biases

Type of Bias	Description	Example
Confirmation bias	The tendency to interpret new evidence as confirmation of one's existing beliefs or theories. This can happen when an interviewer forms a distinct opinion about a candidate based on information obtained outside the interview.	Learning what college the applicant attended and allowing a favorable or unfavorable impression of the school to prejudge the interview, regardless of the candidate's qualifications.
Effective heuristic	Prejudgment of an applicant's superficial attributes, such as visible tattoos or body weight.	An interviewer may make one-dimensional decisions, ignoring more important characteristics, such as problem-solving skills.
Expectation anchor	Relying too heavily on an initial piece of information offered when making decisions.	The interviewer, who really liked one candidate earlier in the process, fails to recognize the superior qualifications of subsequent candidates.
Intuition	Gut decisions	Failure to adequately consider the comparative skill sets of the candidates.
Affinity bias	Tendency to favor others who remind us of ourselves.	Runs the risk of a "clone effect" and unconsciously limits diversity (the tech industry is a prime example).

Lynn Johnson,
Spotlight: Girls—USA

Q: Why did you decide to become a B Corp?

A: The decision to become a B Corp was a no-brainer. I am an entrepreneur who comes from the world of nonprofit arts education and youth development. Since my career started, I have wanted to use my work to make a positive impact on children and families. I started a for-profit business because, as a woman of color, it was crucial for me to also build wealth for myself. So, when I learned of a movement that was all about using business as a force for good in the world, I immediately knew I had found my tribe.

Q: What business benefits do you directly attribute to your B Corp certification?

A: Being a B Corp provides a level of proof to the greater community that we actually walk our talk as an organization. When I tell people that we are a B Corp, their faces light up, either with excited recognition or eager curiosity. Plus, the certification provides a shortcut when connecting with other entrepreneurs. When you meet someone who says, "We're also a B Corp!," you know exactly what that means.

Q: What is your company doing to help build a more inclusive economy?

A: Our business is about supporting the leadership of girls and women. We believe that girls are the leaders our whole world has been waiting for. Being a women of color/LGBT-owned operation that supports other women, we are declaring the importance of centering those of us who have been marginalized in society.

How Can You Implement This at Your Company?

The following are some steps you can take to achieve pay equity.

Develop a compensation rationale.

- Determine what you want to reward (for instance, tenure, responsibility, or performance).
- Develop your job evaluation criteria. This criteria should be specific to your company and relevant to your industry.
- Consider creating an evaluation or compensation committee that has diverse representation itself.

Structure your pay-setting processes objectively.

- Collect job descriptions for all of the roles in your company (including job title and a summary of tasks, responsibilities, and required skills and experience). Ensure that the descriptions use inclusive language and focus on skills needed rather than on personality traits.
- Find out what these jobs are worth in the market. Try to find out what other companies in your industry and geographic area are paying for similar roles.
- Create a job matrix you can use to compare wages, bonuses, and other benefits across positions and determine pay rates for each grade.
- Set and lead with specific pay targets to ensure you're evaluating the job, not just the person filling the job. This will help you to ensure that you aren't under- or overpaying based on previous inequalities (such as if a candidate was paid less at a previous job because of their race, ethnicity, gender, sexual orientation, and so on) or due to unconscious biases.

Conduct a pay equity analysis.

- Identify wage, bonus, or benefit gaps based on gender, race, sexual orientation, age, and so on.
- Understand what needs to be done to create pay equity at your company.
- Set targets and timelines to correct pay inequities.
- Adjust staff members' salaries over time by raising employees' salaries as necessary.
- Consider creating policies that tie executive pay increases or bonuses to pay increases for their staff.
- Be sure to monitor compensation over time to ensure that equity is maintained.

DR. JANA'S TIPS: Some jurisdictions have made it illegal to ask about previous salary. The rationale is that if systemic bias is holding wages down, knowledge of previous wages will facilitate and justify carrying that bias forward into your organization. So, determine whether it is still legal to ask, and consider establishing a policy to not ask and to pay what the job is worth based on experience and other objective criteria. Equal pay for equal work is critical for establishing equitable workplaces. Black women in the United States, for instance, are paid sixty-three cents for every dollar that white men are paid. The ripple effect of this is far-reaching, as 80 percent of black mothers are the income-earning head of their household.[22]

✓ **Determine the multiple that your highest-paid worker earns compared to your lowest-paid full-time worker.**

Why Is This Practice Rewarded?

In 2017, the Economic Policy Institute found that CEOs at the 350 largest companies in America were paid 271 times the annual average salary of the typical worker.[23] Closing this gap can lead to increased employee satisfaction, decreased turnover, and greater shared engagement across the company. Improved wage equity can help to reduce the effect of gender, racial, and other biases associated with a perceived value of work across the company. It also may help facilitate upward mobility for historically marginalized groups.

How Can You Implement This at Your Company?

Some employers have started to implement a cap on the ratio between the highest and lowest earners in their company. Namaste Solar, for example, caps the ratio of its highest salary to its lowest salary at 6:1. Certified B Corps that implement this practice typically cap their pay ratio at between 3:1 and 10:1.

For many companies, the cost of adjusting base compensation to meet a specific highest-to-lowest-wage ratio will be marginal, as the changes would affect only a small number of entry-level employees. Here are some steps you can take to improve in this area.

- **Engage relevant decision makers throughout the process (including the Human Resources department, board members who oversee executive compensation, executives, and directors).** Also consider creating an evaluation committee that is representative of your company across gender, race, ethnicity, disability, sexual orientation, or other groups to guide the process. Begin by discussing how you'll be changing pay ratios and why it's important.

- **Identify the highest- and lowest-paid full-time employees and calculate the multiple, using both wages and bonuses.** Exclude the monetary value of company ownership in your calculations.

- **Discuss a target multiple and develop a plan and timeline for decreasing the wage gap.** This may include increasing pay rates for lowest-paid employees.

- **Consider creating policies that link pay increases or bonus structures for executives with pay increases for their staff.**

- **Tell the story.** Communicate the results of the effort and the expected timeline for adjustments across the company.

DR. JANA'S TIPS: Narrowing the gap in salary ratios can improve employee morale by signaling an increase in authentic, systemic equity—in this case, pay equity. You can expand this even further by ensuring that men and women are paid the same for similar work and that newcomers' salaries don't eclipse that of tenured staff simply because they were hired more recently. Don't be afraid to make equitable salary adjustments. Employees certainly notice when you don't, and it affects their motivation to work by eroding trust over time.

✓ **Create job opportunities for chronically underemployed populations, such as at-risk youth, homeless individuals, or individuals who were formerly incarcerated.**

Example: Greyston Bakery

Greyston Bakery, a Certified B Corporation that is best known for baking the brownies in Ben & Jerry's Chocolate Fudge Brownie ice cream, is located in the impoverished community of Southwest Yonkers, New York. Greyston's open hiring policy offers employment opportunities to anyone, regardless of educational attainment, work history, or previous incarceration, homelessness, or drug use. Anyone who comes to the front door of the bakery is given the chance to work, no questions asked. Greyston provides its workers with resources, personal development tools, and professional training, to give them the greatest chance of success in their new position.

Why Is This Practice Rewarded?

Individuals with a history of incarceration, homelessness, or drug use face many barriers to employment, which may include insufficient job skills, a lack of access to transportation, or disabling health conditions. Individuals who successfully obtain a job may find it difficult to stay employed without access to a wide variety of supportive services. Many veterans, refugees, and people with disabilities face similar barriers.

> *We became a B Corp because we understand that businesses can serve people with disabilities—not just nonprofits or foundations.*
>
> Nicolás Li Calzi, BAU Accesibilidad Universal—Chile

Several innovative B Corporations, such as Cascade Engineering, Daproim Africa, Greyston Bakery, Rivanna Natural Designs, and Rubicon Bakery, provide chronically underemployed individuals with the employment, skills, and resources to lift themselves out of poverty.

How Can You Implement This at Your Company?

Although innovative employment programs take time to build, there are some basic steps that you and your team can take to determine whether a similar partnership is possible for your company.

Many communities already have organizations that work with disabled, homeless, or formerly incarcerated individuals. Reach out to these organizations to see whether they work with local businesses to create employment opportunities for their clients. If there is mutual interest, try offering to help on a short project and/or organizing an employee volunteer day at their facility. This is a great way to help determine whether you and your company are passionate about the organization's cause and whether a more formal partnership would be a good fit.

Many organizations that work with chronically underemployed populations will also help you design, modify, and implement a training program to meet specific needs. For example, Evergreen Lodge, a Certified B Corporation based in California's Yosemite National Park, works with a nonprofit called Juma Ventures to design and implement a summer training program for at-risk youth. Evergreen Lodge's program provides career-oriented training and work experience, includes intensive social services support, and exposes participants to a rich set of outdoor and recreational life experiences.

DR. JANA'S TIPS: Working with the chronically underemployed can increase your company's social capital with constituents, clients, customers, employees, and communities at large by undermining legacies of oppression.

The legacies of white supremacy, slavery, and mass incarceration continue to wreak havoc on black and brown lives in the United States. The U.S. economy was built on the backs of enslaved Africans. Although slavery was not invented in the United States, we added something terrible that helps to explain why blacks in America remain so adversely affected: the United States created generational slavery, thereby cementing a permanent underclass into the fabric of the nation's DNA. We even changed hundreds of years of British patrilineal descendancy laws to matrilineal laws so that the enslaved could not sue for their freedom. If you were born of an enslaved woman, you remained an enslaved person. That law was enacted after a black woman successfully sued for her freedom because her father was the master and he was British. After slavery ended, generational poverty still followed in the wake of Jim Crow laws, systemic racism, redlining, and countless other institutionalized biases designed to keep black and brown people from accessing equality.

We, as B Corps, need to be actively aware of this history. Creating opportunities for vulnerable populations is an extraordinary way to effect authentic change in communities.

✓ **Provide your employees with diversity, equity, and inclusion trainings.**

Why Is This Practice Rewarded?

Providing DEI trainings for staff allows you to move your company toward a culture of shared understanding. This can help your employees feel equipped to
engage thoughtfully and respectfully, without the fear of offending others. It also
can help you to recruit, retain, and empower individuals from historically underrepresented groups and to build a stronger culture of inclusion.

> *Recent research suggests that diversity training that emphasizes legal risk
> and fails to demonstrate senior leadership commitment to diversity often
> backfires. A more effective approach is to have very visible senior leader
> participation. For example, if the CEO or other senior leaders attend all
> diversity trainings and actively participate, that sends a very clear mes-
> sage. Sometimes companies complain that diversity training isn't important
> enough to warrant senior leadership time. That, of course, sends a very
> clear message that the company isn't fully committed to diversity.*

> Gerry Valentine, Vision Executive Coaching—USA

How Can You Implement This at Your Company?

Holding an unconscious bias training is a great place to start. It will help your team understand how unconscious biases work and how they can negatively affect workplace interactions and outcomes. It will also help your team members address and mitigate their own biases. For example, you will need at least a thoughtful, experienced facilitator; leadership and management participation; and actionable objectives. If you need a professional facilitator, Dr. Jana and their team at TMI Consulting are experts in leadership and organizational development and specialize in diversity, equity, and inclusion strategies.

Gather feedback after trainings to make future trainings more effective and to learn what kind of future trainings might interest your employees. These can include racial justice, cultural competency, nonviolent communication, emotional intelligence, cross-cultural team building, and many other trainings.

DR. JANA'S TIPS: Beware the "one and done" trap. It is wholly insufficient to train your group once and then believe that you have made a meaningful contribution. How much do you remember from a given lecture or course? How often are your behaviors impacted and adjusted after just one sitting?

In my first book, *Overcoming Bias*, I use the metaphor of hygiene to explain this phenomenon. Addressing bias, racism, sexism, or any diversity challenge is not like an appendectomy. You don't just cut it out one day and then it's over. It's more like hygiene—you have to keep tending to it if you want to stay healthy. DEI works the same way. And just as you need to have ongoing dialogue about the diversity challenges and inclusion opportunities you experience, you also need to be on the lookout for new data as it emerges.

You can be blindsided if you do not proactively establish a mechanism for communicating with your organization about diversity. I recently changed my pronouns from she/her/hers to they/them/theirs and was able to bring the change to my team in the context of diversity discussions that we have frequently. We've cultivated a safe place for inclusive dialogue. I was a little nervous about sharing my pronoun transition, but my team informed me that they were supportive of standardizing pronoun statements in e-mails and bios across the business. I learned that several of my colleagues' foreign and gender-neutral names cause pronoun confusion and that the mechanism would be helpful even to the cisgendered staff. This would not have happened as smoothly in a workplace where diversity was not a frequent and welcomed topic of discussion.

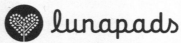

Suzanne Siemens,
Lunapads—Canada

Q: Why did you decide to become a B Corp?

A: We became a founding Canadian B Corp to formalize our long-standing policies and commitments to social justice and environmental benefit. We wanted
to be part of movement to help showcase a better way to do business.

**Q: What business benefits do you directly attribute to your B Corp
certification?**

A: The networking and peer support has been very valuable, from a professional
development perspective. We have also received a good deal of positive PR
and received awards for how well our B Corp values show up in our business
practices.

**Q: What was the biggest challenge you had to overcome to certify as
a B Corp?**

A: We've always operated towards a very high social and environmental standard. To certify, you need to maintain a great deal of rigor to ensure you are
accurately measuring your activities and impact. This requires commitment,
great attention to detail, and dedicated resources to complete.

Q: What was your biggest surprise about becoming a B Corp?

A: I was surprised to find so many tools to help us become better at what we were
already doing or identify things we were not doing well enough. If you are
considering B Corp certification for your business, don't be intimidated. Take
small steps towards getting there. It's worth it!

✓ Offer incentives for employees to organize service days and/or volunteer activities, and set goals to increase the percentage of employees who participate. Communicate your efforts through a written community service policy.

Why Is This Practice Rewarded?

Volunteers provide a tremendous amount of support to nonprofit organizations around the globe. In the United States, for example, roughly 61 million people volunteer annually, at a value of $162 billion.

Companies that measure, compare, and increase the percentage of employees who volunteer in the local community typically provide incentives such as paid time off, company-organized service days, or other perks (such as preferred parking spots) to increase participation.

Creating service and volunteer opportunities for your employees is good for business. The Boston College Center for Corporate Citizenship, for example, reports that employee volunteer programs enhance employee attraction, recruitment, loyalty, and skills as well as a company's image in the community. In addition, according to the study *Good Companies, Better Employees*, employee volunteer programs increase positive word of mouth from employees about their employers, improve worker satisfaction, and increase employee retention rates.[24]

How Can You Implement This at Your Company?

There are many different approaches to encouraging community service at your workplace. The first step is to have a conversation with your employees. Ask them about service opportunities they are most interested in, incentive ideas, how to make volunteering a workplace norm, and similar topics. By engaging your workers in the initial discussions, brainstorming, and creation of the program, you will have a much better chance of strong employee participation. The following are some ideas to help encourage your employees to volunteer:

- Inform employees about volunteer opportunities through bulletin board notices, pay packet inserts, newsletters, intranet, links to volunteer databases, and/or volunteer fairs.
- Offer paid time off specifically to pursue volunteer opportunities.
- Assign a volunteer coordinator to develop and oversee volunteer activities.
- Match individuals who have particular management and technical skills with nonprofit agencies that request help in those areas of expertise.

- Encourage a culture of volunteerism by giving awards to employees for community service.
- Encourage employees to volunteer to sit on a board of directors at a local nonprofit.

We believe that there are many benefits to engaging employees and other company assets in service to the community. However, as we have mentioned elsewhere in this book, these policies and programs need to be evaluated in the

Example: Lunapads's Trans-Inclusive Training for Employees

Lunapads, a B Corp based in Vancouver, Canada, makes healthy, body-positive, eco-friendly personal care products. Suzanne Siemens, cofounder and CEO of Lunapads, describes their experience with a trans-inclusive training for their staff:

> We engaged in trans-inclusive training because we're committed to being a truly feminist business. We all swim in an environment of cisnormative assumptions, and we recognized the need for us, as a team, to recognize the spectrum of diversity around gender and the impact it has on our culture and our business.
>
> The training started out with us looking inward at our own experiences and examining our personal biases. We then discussed ways in which we could look outward, using our voice and business platform to build greater awareness in the community to promote trans inclusion. This included identifying ways in which we were being unintentionally exclusionary in our language and marketing and coming up with immediate ways to improve how we communicated and presented ourselves.
>
> One simple but impactful takeaway from the training was the idea of including our pronouns in our e-mail signatures. Doing so makes a statement to others that we recognize the importance of acknowledging that people's proper pronouns are important and calling them out in our signatures helps normalize it.

context of a larger set of business objectives. For example, financial sustainability of the business needs to be balanced with the positive impact that volunteerism would provide to workers, the local community, the environment, and other stakeholders. One tip would be to start by offering a modest number of paid volunteer hours per year (eight hours is a good starting point). Then set a goal to increase the number of paid volunteer hours every few years. Many B Corps that we have worked with offer twenty-four hours (or three working days) of paid volunteer hours per year.

DR. JANA'S TIPS: Volunteer opportunities are a great way to build relationships and social equity across demographic divides. Even if your company is struggling to hire large numbers of diverse, qualified candidates, volunteer work can put you in direct contact with underrepresented groups. These relationships can help your organization develop a diversity pipeline for recruitment, community engagement, stakeholder programs, and more. Showing up where people are is one of the best ways to build relationship and understanding. This is an opportunity to volunteer for organizations and causes that provide multiple social and environmental benefits. Be sure to source some of the volunteer programs from your employees. People feel included when they get to share their ideas and their personal passions at work.

✓ **Formalize your charitable giving program. Consider creating a partnership with a local charity, matching charitable contributions made by your employees, and joining a third-party organization that certifies charitable giving, such as 1% for the Planet.**

Why Is This Practice Rewarded?

If you and your employees prefer to work with a specific charity, consider creating a formal partnership with that organization. For example, North Coast Brewing Company makes a contribution to marine mammal research for every case of North Coast Steller IPA the company sells. These types of formal partnerships are important because many nonprofits struggle with a lack of consistent donations, which puts pressure on them to focus on short-term fundraising and distracts them from their mission.

For those who are interested in donating money, we highly recommend looking at 1% for the Planet. Members of 1% for the Planet pledge to donate at least 1 percent of their annual sales to one or more environmental nonprofits on an extensive preapproved list. In addition, by joining 1% for the Planet and designating B Lab as your donation recipient, you can offset your B Corp certification fees.[25]

A charity partnership, however, does not have to be limited to financial donations. Your company could donate employee time, free products or services, or allow the charity to use your facilities for trainings or events.

How Can You Implement This at Your Company?

If your company is interested in making financial contributions, we suggest organizing a meeting with your team to discuss creating a written charitable giving policy and a line item in your budget for donations. Even if you have already passed the budgeting process for this year, we recommend having this conversation for next year's budget.

Another good idea is to ask your employees or customers where they are donating already. Choosing a cause that your stakeholders already care about will get everyone excited and will lead to better participation in your campaign.

DR. JANA'S TIPS: Be mindful not to make the charitable giving program a vehicle of exclusion. Sometimes organizational leaders mean well and create competitions and programs to incentivize giving in a very visible way. This creates undue stress for people who do not have the disposable income to contribute. You have to remember that the massive wealth gap between white people and people of color in the United States is such that most black and Hispanic families do not have access to savings, family money, trusts, investments, or other liquid assets beyond their paychecks. Charitable giving competitions can create a particular social pressure when not thoughtfully implemented. Also ask how your charitable giving contributes to local self-reliance and community ownership. Who gets to pick where your money is donated? Are employees involved? Is the selection process transparent, objective, and fair?

Example: North Coast Brewing Company

North Coast Brewing Company, a B Corp craft brewery located in Northern California, created an employee volunteering program in 2016 to inspire and encourage people to creatively engage in their local communities, and to recognize them for doing so. North Coast first partnered with another local B Corp, Harvest Market, to learn about key elements of successful volunteering programs. The companies knew that by joining forces and encouraging each business to develop its own volunteering initiative, they could have double the impact in their local community.

North Coast surveyed its employees to learn more about what types of volunteering they were involved in and excited about. Then the company created a policy to encourage and recognize volunteer participation. Within a few months of program launch, 17.5 percent of employees reported volunteer hours. Volunteer activities included participating in a local beach cleanup day, serving on nonprofit boards of directors, and helping at nonprofit fundraising events throughout Mendocino County. After establishing a baseline, North Coast Brewing Company set a 20 percent employee participation goal to encourage its team to continue to make a positive impact in the future.

✓ **Purchase from local suppliers or from suppliers owned by women, people of color, or individuals from other underrepresented populations.**

Why Is This Practice Rewarded?

Purchasing from companies owned by women, people of color, veterans, or ex-offenders, or from companies located in low-income communities can benefit a wide variety of stakeholders. For example, purchasing local goods and services from underrepresented entrepreneurs will support job creation within your community, will keep tax dollars invested in community projects, will reduce the environmental impact of long-distance shipping, and will support individuals who have been subject to systemic biases and discrimination.

How Can You Implement This at Your Company?

Here are a number of steps you can take to improve your performance in this area.

- **Consider developing a preferential supplier policy that prioritizes suppliers owned by women and/or other underrepresented individuals.** Your policy should align with your company's social and environmental values and priorities.

- **Collect information about the ownership of your current suppliers through a supplier survey and/or supplier interviews.** (This can be done in conjunction with broader supplier screens.) Screen for third-party certifications such as women and/or minority ownership.

- **Analyze your supplier data and develop a plan and timeline to incorporate new suppliers who meet your criteria.**

- **Create an internal supplier directory resource that includes information on diversity-of-ownership metrics.** Consider creating a supplier checklist for all employees engaging with suppliers. Hold employees accountable for using the checklist.

DR. JANA'S TIPS: Economic empowerment is a vital tool for increasing opportunity, wealth, access, and well-being for marginalized communities. Purchasing from diverse suppliers is a strong step toward righting the historical wrongs that continue to keep underrepresented groups on the margins of society. Economic empowerment is tantamount to freedom. Your purchase contract with a small, underrepresented company can make the difference between a college education for a child and a lifetime of student loan debt, between owning a home and renting a home, or between economic security and living paycheck to paycheck.

If it is too much of a challenge or a risk to move towards transformational diversity, equity, and inclusion at your own business, try first to outsource to companies who are doing it well. Even if you end up outsourcing indefinitely, you have still achieved the objective of including underrepresented groups in your business.

Thomas Ng, founder, Genashtim Innovative Learning—Malaysia

✓ **Use a formal, written supplier code of conduct that specifically holds the company's suppliers accountable for social and environmental performance.**

Why Is This Practice Rewarded?

A supplier code of conduct will help to ensure that the companies you do business with are accountable to guidelines of performance, safety, and transparency. Supplier codes of conduct are of special importance if your company sources a majority of its products from countries with uneven or lax enforcement of environmental, labor, and human rights laws.

How Can You Implement This at Your Company?

The first step is to assess your company's supply chain risks. In particular, you should ask the following questions:

- Where do you source your manufactured products from?
- How are environmental and human rights laws enforced in your country of operations?
- Do you manufacture products that require the use of toxic chemicals?
- Do the methods that are being used to produce your products conflict with the stated social or environmental objectives of your company?

There are several approaches to monitoring your supplier code of conduct. These options include self-audits by your supplier, site visits by an internal team, and/or site visits by a third party. The approach you take depends on your company's budget, your assessment of the probability that your suppliers may be engaged in unethical practices, and your suppliers' willingness to be transparent.

Finally, your supplier code of conduct should describe what happens if any violations to your code are discovered. Issues to consider include:

- the circumstances under which you would stop working with a supplier;
- how long a supplier has to remedy a problem that is discovered;
- whether your company or audit firm wants to play an active role in helping your supplier solve the problem that led to the violation;
- what happens if there is a repeat offense; and
- whether you will make the discovery of any violations public

Visit the LIFT Economy website for great examples of codes of conduct for suppliers from B Corps like Patagonia and MaCher.[26]

DR. JANA'S TIPS: There are many ways to create positive change. No matter the size of your company, you have some level of purchasing power to promote inclusion in your supply chain. Obviously, larger companies can be seen as having the scale and influence necessary to nudge suppliers toward improvement. However, both large and small companies, especially as part of a collective like the B Corp community, have the potential to create an outsize positive impact on society and the environment by holding suppliers to the same basic standards of conduct to which we hold our own enterprises.

✓ **Bank with a local independent bank or credit union. Choose a bank that is a Certified B Corporation, a community development financial institution, or a member of the Global Alliance for Banking on Values.**

Why Is This Practice Rewarded?

Voting with your dollars extends beyond responsible purchasing decisions. It is also important to think about where you keep your money—and how your money is being invested.

Many locally owned banks and credit unions offer the same array of services as big banks, from online bill paying to debit and credit cards, at a lower cost. In addition, loan approvals and other decisions are made by people who live in the community, have face-to-face relationships with their customers, and understand local needs. Because of this personal knowledge, local financial institutions are often able to approve loans that big banks would reject.

How Can You Implement This at Your Company?

If you are considering switching banks, there are a number of questions to ask prospective financial institutions, including:

- Do you have any socially or environmentally responsible banking practices?
- Are there any industries in which you specialize?
- Are there any industries that you avoid?
- What size company do you most often finance and serve?
- Do you participate in the Small Business Administration loan program?
- Are you a member of the Global Alliance for Banking on Values?

DR. JANA'S TIPS: Local independent banks and credit unions tend to have more sustainable, favorable options for small, women-owned, and minority-owned businesses. This makes such banks tremendous community assets, so supporting them helps create economic equity and inclusion for people who might otherwise not be able to grow their businesses. Banks that lend locally can be more flexible with terms and collateral. The larger banks tend to sell their loans and have much stricter requirements for smaller, less-advantaged clientele.

✓ **Publicly disclose the names of your suppliers (and their social and environmental performance).**

Why Is This Practice Rewarded?

This practice rewards businesses that promote safe working conditions, treat workers with respect and dignity, and/or use environmentally responsible manufacturing processes. Supply chain transparency is especially important if your company sources a majority of its products from developing countries, where enforcement of environmental and labor laws can vary widely.

In addition, consumers are increasingly curious about where and how their products are made. A report by Cohn & Wolfe states, "Transparency has become more important in the past year, and now stands alongside quality and price in the decision-making process for consumers." Supply chain transparency is particularly important for businesses, given the rise of social media and readier availability of information. Cohn & Wolfe found that "half of consumers would stop buying a product or a service if they found out the company did not reflect their personal values, whilst 30 percent would encourage their friends and families to do the same. A quarter would go even further and support a boycott of the company."[27]

How Can You Implement This at Your Company?

The first step toward improving supply chain transparency is to do a baseline assessment of your supply chain's overall social and environmental performance. In our opinion, the best (free) means of benchmarking this performance is to ask your suppliers to take the B Impact Assessment.[28]

Set goals to increase your supply chain transparency over time. Increased transparency can help you generate consumer trust, improve your brand value, and build leadership in your industry. Encourage and assist your suppliers in pursuing third-party certification. This can benefit your company by increasing independent, verified accountability within your supply chain and can benefit your supplier by helping it attract more mission-aligned customers.

Example: Fairphone

Fairphone, a mobile phone producer based in the Netherlands, is working to create a fairer supply chain focused on the mining, design, manufacturing, and life cycle of its products. Fairphone has created a digital map of its suppliers to understand the origination of its raw materials and strives to improve the social and environmental conditions of each step in its supply chain.

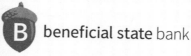
beneficial state bank

Kat Taylor,
Beneficial State Bank—USA

Q: Why did you decide to become a B Corp?

A: We initially took the B Impact Assessment with the help of a student team from the Presidio Graduate School. The assessment gave us enormous insights into what we were doing well and what we could do better. The process really stimulated our natural sense of "coopetition" (to use a credit union term). Since becoming a B Corp we have recognized that the community is one of our strongest associations, providing strength in numbers in what is essentially a movement to bend business toward becoming a universal force for good.

Q: What business benefits do you directly attribute to your B Corp certification?

A: B Corp status and community membership yields many practical benefit: a great certification to discipline our own supply chain and procurement practices, fellow travelers to seek advice or solace or celebration along the way, and of course discounts and partnerships that hit our bottom line directly.

Q: What is your company doing to help build a more inclusive economy?

A: Our whole thesis is that banking is the original and most powerful form of crowdfunding. If banking really belongs to us all and funds the world in which we live, we need only reclaim our agency (our choice) and our accountability (our responsibility) over where our money sleeps at night to be part of crowdfunding a better world for all. While this idea can be seen as inherently inclusive, we hold diversity and inclusion as a strong and explicit value in our culture in order to counter the historic discrimination and economic realities that bar so many from participating in banking.

DR. JANA'S TIPS: If you have taken the time to engage diverse suppliers, listing them on your website with an assessment of their social and environmental performance elevates your brand and your social capital. Your transparency can encourage other companies to follow suit, and it shows your stakeholders that your commitment to multiple social values is authentic and verifiable.

A lot of organizations boast about the good they do. Sometimes all you need to do is to show people what you are really about. It also creates opportunities for accountability. If a company you have listed is engaging in disreputable, noninclusive practices, a public presence allows constituents the opportunity to inform your leadership about the concern. I have seen this occur with increasing frequency around the #MeToo movement. People do not wish to see B Corp brands tarnished by unethical behavior, so when they have access to your resource and vendor lists, they can help you avoid embarrassment by association.

✓ **Work within your industry to develop social and environmental standards.**

Why Is This Practice Rewarded?

In addition to rewarding individual improvements, the B Impact Assessment acknowledges businesses that advocate reforms in their industries. There often are stronger commitments and higher rates of adoption when change is led by businesses within a given sector.

There are many ways that you can improve your industry's overall social and environmental performance. For example, you could serve on a working group to help educate your peers, advocate the adoption of voluntary environmental reporting standards, or help pass legislation that creates incentives for businesses to improve their performance.

How Can You Implement This at Your Company?

Research the various trade associations in your sector. There is a good chance that there are already some social and environmental initiatives within your industry. Contact other businesses and get involved. If there is no existing sustainability initiative, start one.

Another excellent step would be to get involved with existing organizations that promote social and environmental responsibility. In the United States, examples include the American Sustainable Business Council, the Business Alliance for Local Living Economies, the Fair Labor Association, Fairtrade International, Green America, the Green Chamber of Commerce, and Social Venture Network.

DR. JANA'S TIPS: If the leaders in your industry don't have DEI standards or benchmarks, your company should lead the way. As B Corps, we are the standard bearers for using the power of business as a force for good. I believe that B Corps are poised to change the world for the better through intentional, concerted effort. If no one is leading the way in diverse and equitable practices in your industry, why shouldn't your company take on the challenge? TMI Consulting can help you develop a strategy to achieve your goals.

Quick Assessment of Environmental Impact

Want to get an idea of how good your company is for the environment? Take the following twelve-item Quick Assessment to measure your performance over the past year. You can add up your total at the bottom for a rough idea of how you might score on the Environment section of the B Impact Assessment.

Check the box if you and/or your company . . .

☐ monitor, record, and reduce your greenhouse gas emissions.

☐ use energy-efficient lighting systems (e.g., natural light, LEDs, CFLs, occupancy sensors, daylight dimmers, or task lighting), office equipment (e.g., Energy Star appliances, automatic sleep modes, or after-hours timers), and heating and air-conditioning systems (e.g., programmable thermostats, timers, occupancy sensors, or double-paned windows).

☐ use water-efficient systems (e.g., low-flow toilets, faucets, or showerheads) or harvest rainwater.

☐ use low-impact renewable energy.

☐ purchase renewable energy credits to offset any nonrenewable energy that you use.

☐ provide employees with incentives to use alternative commuting options to get to work.

☐ encourage employees to use virtual meeting technology to reduce travel.

☐ conduct life cycle assessments of your products.

☐ create a reclamation project to recycle or reuse end products.

☐ have an environmental purchasing policy for office supplies, food, electronics, cleaning products, product input materials, and other items, as appropriate.

☐ responsibly dispose of hazardous waste (e.g., batteries, paint, or electronic equipment).

☐ have a written policy requiring inbound and outbound freight or shipping to be transported via the lowest-impact methods possible (e.g., avoiding shipment by air transport).

_____ **Total**

Give yourself one point for each affirmative response.

If you scored from zero to 3, you will have some work do to earn B Corp certification. Alternatively, you can make up ground with an outstanding performance in the other areas.

If you scored from 4 to 6, you are a good candidate for B Corp certification, assuming you perform similarly well on the other sections.

If you scored from 7 to 12, fantastic work! You are likely well on your way to getting the score you need for B Corp certification.

Environment

Being good for the environment is good for your company's bottom line. Many businesses, such as Ben & Jerry's, Method, and Patagonia, have found that improving their environmental performance has increased their profits by helping them attract top talent, create more durable relationships with suppliers, and increase consumer trust.

How we treat the environment directly affects historically marginalized communities. The consequences of climate change for health, housing, livelihood, and security disproportionately affects Indigenous communities, women, elderly individuals, those with disabilities, the incarcerated, and the poor. For instance, low-income individuals and people of color disproportionately bear the negative economic, environmental, and health impacts of the fossil fuel economy at every stage of its life cycle, including its exploration, extraction, production, refining, distribution, consumption, and waste disposal.

The environmental justice movement was founded more than 30 years ago to address this inequity. Environmental justice is defined as the fair treatment and meaningful involvement of all people, regardless of race, color, national origin, or income, with respect to environmental laws. Fair treatment means that no group of people should bear a disproportionate share of the negative environmental consequences of certain programs or decisions. Simply put, environmental justice means that everyone (not just the people who can "vote with their feet" and move away from threats, or individuals who can afford lawyers, experts, and lobbyists to fight on their behalf) is entitled to equal protection and equal enforcement of our environmental, health, housing, land use, transportation, energy, and civil rights laws and regulations.

✓ **Monitor, record, and reduce your greenhouse gas emissions.**

Why Is This Practice Rewarded?

Gases that trap heat in the atmosphere are called greenhouse gases. Monitoring, recording, and reducing your GHG emissions can help your company save money, save energy, and ease pressure on planetary life. Because greenhouse gas emissions are closely linked to energy use, measuring emissions can lead to identifying ways to reduce those emissions and increase savings.

One of the best-researched, extensive, and comprehensive attempts to identify solutions to reduce GHG emissions is Project Drawdown. Project Drawdown's goal is to gather the best available information on climate solutions in order to illustrate their beneficial financial, social, and environmental impact over the next thirty years. The

Drawdown team gathered a qualified and diverse group of researchers from around the world to identify, research, and model the one hundred most substantive existing solutions to address climate change. Solutions range from clean energy to educating girls in lower-income countries to land use practices that pull carbon out of the air.

The solutions exist and they are economically viable, and communities throughout the world are already implementing them. If deployed collectively on a global scale over the next thirty years, these solutions represent a credible path forward, not just to slow the earth's warming but to reach drawdown, the point at which greenhouse gases in the atmosphere peak and then begin to decline. These measures promise cascading benefits to human health, security, prosperity, and well-being—giving us a reason to see this planetary crisis as an opportunity to create a just and livable world.

The objective of the list of one hundred solutions is to be inclusive, presenting an extensive array of effective measures already in existence. The list comprises primarily "no regrets" solutions—actions that make sense to take regardless of their positive climate impact because they provide intrinsic benefits to communities and economies. These initiatives improve lives, create jobs, restore the environment, enhance security, generate resilience, and advance human health.

The top ten solutions to reversing climate change, ranked in order of most to least atmospheric CO_2 reduction potential, include refrigerant management (that is, controlling leaks of refrigerants from existing appliances like air conditioners); onshore wind turbines; reducing food waste; converting more people to a plant-rich diet; reforesting and protecting tropical-climate forests; educating girls (women with more years of education have fewer and healthier children); family planning (securing women's right to family planning can have positive impacts on health, welfare, and life expectancy); utility-scale solar farms; silvopasture (the addition of trees to grassland pastures for increased productivity and sequestration of carbon); and rooftop solar. You can find the other ninety solutions, plus extensive technical reports and financial models, at the Drawdown website.[29]

How Can You Implement This at Your Company?

Calculating emissions is a multistep process. The Greenhouse Gas Protocol is the most widely used international accounting tool for government and business leaders to understand, quantify, and manage greenhouse gas emissions. The GHG Protocol Initiative provides the accounting framework for nearly every GHG standard and program in the world as well as hundreds of GHG inventories prepared by individual companies. GHG Protocol's tool set enables companies to develop comprehensive and reliable inventories of their GHG emissions.

For small businesses, Certified B Corp Carbon Analytics can help you calculate your company's carbon footprint for free. TripZero, another B Corp, can help you offset the carbon footprint of your business travel for free.[30]

✓ **Use low-impact renewable energy. Purchase renewable energy credits to offset any nonrenewable energy that you use.**

Why Is This Practice Rewarded?

Not all types of renewable energy are created equal. For example, although hydropower does not create emissions in the production of energy, large-scale dams can cause other environmental and social problems. This is why the B Impact Assessment rewards companies that choose low-impact renewable energy sources. Examples include electricity and heat generated from solar, wind, ocean, low-impact hydropower, biomass, geothermal, or hydrogen resources. You may already receive a percentage of renewable energy from your utility provider. In Northern California, for example, approximately 33 percent of electricity provided by the local utility is derived from renewable sources, which will earn you points on the B Impact Assessment.

How Can You Implement This at Your Company?

If you do not have an on-site source of renewable energy (such as solar panels, wind, or a geothermal system), or if your local utility provider does not have a green power program, you can purchase renewable energy credits to offset your carbon emissions. When looking at purchasing renewable energy certificates, consider variables like price, percentage of renewable energy, percentage of new or incremental renewable sources, renewable energy mix, and third-party certification and verification. B Corps 3Degrees and Native Energy are great resources for companies looking for more information on renewable energy credits, carbon offsets, and more.[31]

DR. JANA'S TIPS: When purchasing carbon offsets or renewable energy credits, try to support organizations that also work with low-income communities, people of color, or other marginalized groups. BioCarbon Partners (highlighted below) is a great example. It is possible to promote diversity, equity, and inclusion and reduce your environmental impact at the same time.

Taryn Lane,
Hepburn Wind—Australia

Q: Why did you decide to become a B Corp?

A: The B Corp idea is a match in values for us because it formalizes our ethics in a way that is broader than our existing cooperative principles.

Q: What business benefits do you directly attribute to your B Corp certification?

A: It holds us accountable into the future. We sell our electricity and carbon offset product to other B Corps and look to utilize services from the B Corp community.

Q: What was your biggest surprise about becoming a B Corp?

A: We were most surprised by how well our model had been set up and evolved over time. We scored very highly on the B Impact Assessment, which was a metaphorical pat on the back for all of the amazing volunteers and staff that have all made our wind farm what it is today.

Q: What is your company doing to help build a more inclusive economy?

A: As a community-based cooperative, we are here to share the benefits of the wind farm and lead our community's transition to zero-net emissions. This means considering our entire community and how to provide them with opportunities to both participate and benefit. We have a community fund which has provided grants to over fifty local community groups over the past six years. We also have an energy fund that supports things like EV [electric vehicle] charging stations, solar on community buildings, solar bulk buys, and grid-connected solar farms. Community energy keeps the local economy growing.

✓ **Provide employees with incentives to use alternative commuting options to get to work. Instead of traveling for work, encourage employees to use virtual meeting technology whenever possible.**

Why Is This Practice Rewarded?

Employers that encourage alternative commuting, such as carpooling, vanpooling, use of public transit, bicycling, or telework, reduce carbon emissions by keeping cars off the road. Moreover, such employers have been shown to have happier workers, enhanced job performance, and higher employee retention rates.[32]

According to the Climate Disclosure Project, an individual business implementing virtual meeting technology in four of its meeting rooms can reduce its CO_2 emissions by 2,271 metric tons over five years. These reductions are equivalent to the annual greenhouse gas emissions from more than four hundred passenger vehicles.[33]

How Can You Implement This at Your Company?

Engage your employees in a discussion about alternative commuting. The key is to keep trying new ideas, to solicit feedback, and to continue to adjust as needed. The following few questions may help start the conversation:

☐ Will subsidies or financial incentives for alternative commuting be provided?

☐ Will nonfinancial incentives such as prizes and awards be offered?

☐ Is there a need to construct new facilities, such as showers for bicyclists?

☐ Can the company work with existing regional transit services, such as ride matching or a Guaranteed Ride Home program, or is there a need to coordinate those internally?

- [ ] How much staff time will be required to administer the program?

- [ ] Are employment levels at your company expected to change in the next few years? The answer to this question may help you plan your initiative to better meet future trends.

- [ ] Are there clusters of employees with common commute characteristics (such as home location and arrival/departure times)? This information can be helpful for employees who are looking for rideshare matches.

- [ ] Which alternative commuting options are employees most willing to try? Survey your employees to find out.

DR. JANA'S TIPS: Be mindful of the realities that historically marginalized groups face with regard to transportation to and from work. For instance, perhaps an employee from an underrepresented group needs their car to drive to a second job. Perhaps the person does not have a computer with quick enough internet speed at home to have video calls. Bicycling, while undoubtedly good for one's health and better for the environment, may not be a realistic possibility if someone lives in a lower-income neighborhood farther away from the office. Or maybe none of these is true and the person is one of your most enthusiastic participants in alternative commuting solutions. The point is to better understand what is realistic and unrealistic for all of your staff. Try reaching out to folks individually and having a discussion.

✓ **Conduct a life cycle assessment of your products.**

Why Is This Practice Rewarded?

A life cycle assessment helps a company to see the complete picture of its products' environmental impact. For a typical product, an LCA takes into account the acquisition of raw materials, transport, manufacturing, product packaging, the use of the product, and disposal of the product and its packaging after use. LCAs have been done on a variety of products, including jet engines, diapers, drinking cups, and computers.

There are many reasons for your company to conduct a life cycle assessment. It can be used to reduce your environmental footprint, eliminate waste, reduce costs, support marketing claims, or improve your brand's image. An LCA also creates common metrics that can be compared and shared with your employees, suppliers, and partners.

We decided to conduct an LCA because we wanted to better know where to prioritize our sustainability efforts and our focus. For example, we use stand-up, flexible plastic bags to sell our foods—mostly because they help to guarantee their freshness for a longer time. However, a common perception among our customers is that packaging is our greatest problem (when, in fact, it's not). The LCA revealed that packaging only accounted for 5 percent of our environmental impact, whereas the agricultural practices of our suppliers were responsible for around 80 percent. In this way, the study has shown us that we need to better inform our customers about our hot spots and, most importantly, communicate what we're doing to address them. The LCA has allowed PRANA to set relevant priorities for an action plan that is credible but also relevant to everyone's overall long-term success.

Tiffanie Murillo, PRANA—Canada

How Can You Implement This at Your Company?

Completing a life cycle assessment is a very in-depth process and may require more technical expertise or time commitment than your business can provide. In this instance, you may decide to hire a consultant to assist you in conducting an LCA. The cost of outsourcing your LCA will vary depending on the nature of the assessment, the availability of existing data, and the number of alternative products you want to compare.

DR. JANA'S TIPS: Beyond all the environmental aspects of your product throughout its life cycle, how does the production, manufacturing, and disposal of your product impact historically marginalized groups? The vast majority of LCAs (if not all) do not take this into account. Will you be one of the first to consider this additional layer of impact? How can you start to map DEI onto your product life cycle?

✓ **Create a reclamation project to recycle or reuse end products.**

Why Is This Practice Rewarded?

This practice rewards companies that accept the return of their products for environmentally responsible reuse, recycling, or disposal. Product reclamation is important because many municipalities are not equipped to handle anything beyond the standard paper, glass, plastic, and aluminum.

SISTEMA.bio®
CREATING VALUE FROM WASTE

Xunaxi Cruz,
Sistema Biobolsa—Mexico

Q: What business benefits do you directly attribute to your B Corp certification?

A: Our mission as a social business is an equitable, empathic, and sustainable world without waste. We manufacture, sell, and install a biodigester that transforms animal waste into renewable resources (biogas and a rich organic fertilizer) for small farmers. Being a B Corp shows that we belong to the most important community of change markers in the world. This has attracted impact investment, talent, and new business development opportunities. We are recognized as an international example of a sustainable enterprise.

Q: If you could change one thing about the B Corp movement, what would it be?

A: We are proud pioneers of the Mexican B Corp community. We would like to invite more businesses from the areas we work—such as Latin America, India, and the African continent—to the B Corp movement. While the B Corp community has been growing, we believe there is much more that B Corps can do to make this world a better place.

Q: What advice do you have for a business that is considering B Corp certification?

A: This certification should be a commitment to always have the highest standards of quality, service, and positive impact. No matter how big your company gets, B Corp can help you keep track of your goals of creating a new economy and using business as a force for good.

In response to the challenge of recycling different materials, many countries have started to experiment with extended producer responsibility programs, through which producers are held responsible for the costs of managing their products at the end of their usable life. The theory behind extended producer responsibility is that the producer has the greatest control over the original product design, which in turn gives it the greatest ability and responsibility to deal with its used products.

How Can You Implement This at Your Company?

The steps your company takes to implement a reclamation program will largely depend on your industry, location, and company size. To identify next steps, research existing programs in your area, discuss possibilities with employees, seek feedback from a wide range of stakeholders, and consider starting a small pilot project before launching a formal program. One of the best ways to learn more is to reach out to some of the Certified B Corps that have product reclamation programs in place. Most B Corps will be happy to share their experiences and to advise you on next steps. Patagonia's Worn Wear initiative and Preserve's Gimme 5 program are notable leaders in this area.

DR. JANA'S TIPS: It is critical to reduce the amount of waste going to landfills. Landfills, hazardous waste sites, and other industrial facilities are most often located in communities of color, causing a range of health and environmental damage. This is an environmental justice issue that you and your company can get involved with. If you do decide to create a product take-back program, this can be a great opportunity to hire chronically underserved populations such as formerly incarcerated and/or formerly homeless individuals. These jobs usually are relatively straightforward and involve working with one's hands—skill sets that almost anyone can learn.

✓ **Create an environmental purchasing policy for office supplies, food, electronics, cleaning products, product input materials, and other items, as appropriate.**

Why Is This Practice Rewarded?

An environmental purchasing policy can help encourage your staff to use environmental responsibility as a factor in their purchasing decisions. In particular, a formal policy can help guide staff to consider goods and services that can be manufactured, used, and disposed of in an environmentally responsible way; to give preference, where items are of a similar cost, to those that are manufactured with a high recycled content; to specify items that can be recycled or reused; to consider the energy usage and cost of operating equipment prior to purchase; to favor suppliers that are committed to environmental improvement; and to consider "whole life" costs and impacts when assessing equipment for purchase.

How Can You Implement This at Your Company?

If you decide to create a new policy, start with an overview of your company's goals and objectives for purchasing. For example, you might state, "Our company is committed to forging supplier relationships that lead to positive outcomes for society and the environment. Therefore, we have developed this policy to encourage the purchase and use of materials, products, and services that incorporate environmental, social, community, and performance goals."

Next, you might consider some language addressing the value of third-party certification for vendors. An example would be "Preference will be given to suppliers that meet robust third-party social and environmental certification criteria. Examples of this third-party certifications that we will value include, but are not limited to, B Corp, Certified Organic, Energy Star, Fairtrade, Food Alliance, Green Seal, Just Business, LEED, and Non-GMO Project. Other rigorous and independent third-party certifications will be considered on a case by case basis."

DR. JANA'S TIPS: In addition to purchasing products or services that are environmentally friendly, try to purchase from suppliers that are owned by and/or support historically marginalized groups. This will help support progress on DEI while reducing your impact on the planet.

✓ **Responsibly dispose of hazardous waste such as batteries, paint, or electronic equipment.**

Why Is This Important?

Hazardous waste is dangerous or potentially harmful to our health or the environment. Responsible disposal of hazardous materials isn't just the domain of heavy manufacturing. Professional offices, too, must pay attention to disposal of janitorial supplies, building materials, and electronic waste. Improper hazardous waste disposal can harm the health of employees, local residents, and the environment. It can contaminate soil or the local water supply and pollute the air. It also can lead to a decrease in property value and expose your business to fines and/or lawsuits.

How Can You Implement This at Your Company?

There are a few steps to eliminating, reducing, and/or properly disposing of hazardous waste. First, try to prevent hazardous waste during the production process, rather than jumping straight to disposal. Second, if you've tried to reduce waste production but still have hazardous waste, see if your town, city, or county offers hazardous waste collection. Collection will make waste disposal easier for you and will ensure that your business follows disposal regulations. Finally, proper disposal of hazardous waste depends on the type of waste. Research your local waste management authority to identify what types of waste are accepted in your area.

DR. JANA'S TIPS: It is incredibly important to properly dispose of hazardous waste, but where does it go once you have disposed of it? As I already mentioned, landfills, hazardous waste sites, and other industrial facilities are most often located in communities of color. People of color are nearly twice as likely as white residents to live within the "fenceline" zone of an industrial facility. These facilities contribute to air pollution, safety issues, and health concerns.

Perhaps the best thing you can do is to try to reduce the amount of hazardous waste your company creates in the first place. Once you have tried that, identify where your hazardous waste is currently sent. Are there any proposals in your region to build a new waste or industrial facility in a location that is predominantly poor or predominantly home to people of color? If so, resist it. Use your voice (and your privilege) to stand up for these communities.

✓ **Create a low-impact transportation, distribution, and shipping policy.**

Why Is This Practice Rewarded?

Ray Anderson, late founder and CEO of Interface and a corporate sustainability leader, once said, "The greenest gallon of gas, diesel, heating oil, or ton of coal is the one you don't burn." You can swap the word "greenest" with the word "cheapest" and the same holds true. With one-quarter of the trucks on U.S. and British highways traveling empty on any given day, companies are looking for opportunities to reduce transportation overall—from eliminating empty space in their transportation chains to data management systems that enable more detailed planning.[34] This helps move the same goods with fewer trips and reduces spending on fuel, fleet maintenance, and/or contracting with vendors.

How Can You Implement This at Your Company?

Creating a low-impact transportation and distribution policy is a great way to encourage resource efficiency. First, start with why you are making a policy. For example, you might state, "Our organization has developed this transportation and distribution policy to reduce carbon emissions from the shipment and distribution of both inbound and outbound freight."

Second, describe what this will look like in practice—for instance, "We will select and work with shippers and distributors to ensure that inbound and outbound freight is shipped via the lowest-impact methods feasible (such as by avoiding air transport). This may include using shipping companies that utilize alternative fuels in their trucks and/or require full loads for transport."

Quick Assessment of Governance Impact

Want to get an idea of how good your company is for the environment? Take the following twelve-item Quick Assessment to measure your performance over the past year. You can add up your total at the bottom for a rough idea of how you might score on the Environment section of the B Impact Assessment.

Check the box if you and/or your company . . .

- ☐ integrate a commitment to social and/or environmental responsibility into your written corporate mission statement.

- ☐ train employees on your social and/or environmental mission.

- ☐ evaluate employees and management on their performance with regard to your company's social and environmental targets.

- ☐ tie social and environmental performance to bonuses or other rewards.

- ☐ solicit from your external stakeholders (customers, community members, suppliers, or nonprofit organizations) feedback about your company's social and environmental performance.

- ☐ maintain a board of directors, advisory board, or other governing body that includes women, people of color, LGBTQIA individuals, and other under-represented individuals.

- ☐ include nonexecutive employees, community members, and environmental experts on your board of directors.

- [ ] ensure that your board reviews your company's social and environmental performance on an annual basis.

- [ ] share with your employees basic financial information.

- [ ] produce an external annual report detailing your mission-related performance.

- [ ] have legally institutionalized your mission in your corporate structure (for instance, by inserting a stakeholder consideration into your governing documents or by incorporating as a benefit corporation).

_____ **Total**

Give yourself one point for each affirmative response.

If you scored from zero to 3, you will have some work do to earn B Corp certification. Alternatively, you can make up ground with an outstanding performance in the other areas.

If you scored from 4 to 6, you are a good candidate for B Corp certification, assuming you perform similarly well on the other sections.

If you scored from 7 to 11, fantastic work! You are likely well on your way to getting the score you need for B Corp certification.

Governance

Patagonia's Yvon Chouinard says he wants to build a company that will last for one hundred years. King Arthur Flour—a two-hundred-year-old company—became a B Corp so the company has a better chance to thrive for another two hundred years. If you are going to build a better business, it is important that it can survive changes in management and ownership.

As we have seen, it can be challenging to build a business that is good for workers, good for the community, and good for the environment. It can be even more challenging to build a business that is good for the long term.

B Corps believe that one of the keys to durability is to bake your mission into your company's cultural and legal DNA. This involves making your mission come to life by increasing shared accountability for your company's long-term success. It means integrating your values into job descriptions, performance reviews, and even your corporate governing documents. It also means being transparent, open, and honest about your company's mission-related performance and how your company can do better in the future.

To help you on your journey, we will highlight some of these topics, discuss why they are important, explain why they are rewarded on the assessment, and offer tips for implementing these practices in your company.

✓ **Integrate a commitment to social and/or environmental responsibility into your written corporate mission statement.**

Why Is This Practice Rewarded?

Vision, mission, and values are the foundation of your business. Creating an explicit commitment to social and environmental responsibility can help your business stay purpose-driven, especially through changes in employees, ownership, and management. Many B Corps have found that this is one of the most important things they have done to create internal alignment within their organizations.

How Can You Implement This at Your Company?

If you want to create a vision/mission/values statement for your business, get your board of directors, management team, and employees together and follow the prompts outlined here. Involve as many people as you can.

1. **Vision.** Ask yourself, "What do we want to become?" A vision statement should succinctly describe what your company will look like in five years—for example, "We are nationally recognized as one of the top thought leaders in coaching and strategy for social entrepreneurs."

2. **Mission.** Ask yourself, "What kind of business are we in?" Your mission statement should provide a clear, concise description of your organization's overall purpose. This can enable large groups of individuals to work in a unified direction toward a common cause. A good mission statement should be challenging yet achievable. Patagonia's mission statement, for example, is "Build the best product, cause no unnecessary harm, use business to inspire and implement solutions to the environmental crisis." Method's mission statement is "To inspire a happy and healthy home revolution." LIFT Economy's mission statement is "To create, model, and share an inclusive and locally self-reliant economy that works for the benefit of all life."

3. **Values.** Ask yourself, "What do we stand for?" The statement of values ties the vision and mission together. It provides the decision-making filter for how the business will conduct its activities while carrying out its mission and vision.

DR. JANA'S TIPS: Companies often forget to include a vision that defines the employee experience. Our employees typically are one of the greatest assets a company has. Why allow company culture to define itself?

When TMI Consulting helps clients with diversity, equity, and inclusion initiatives, we often find ourselves having to define an organizational culture for the first time. Don't wait for something to happen that doesn't represent your company values. Be proactive in defining the workplace experience for employees. Describe how you expect people to be treated. Describe how people should feel *at* work and *about* their work. It's great to talk about how we want the customer to feel, but try not to exclude the employee experience. Define it, codify it, and teach it to all new employees. That way, if something does go wrong within the culture, you can refer back to the aspirational vision you created. Consider cocreating that vision with employees so that they have a sense of ownership of the final vision. Then, as you add new programs, goals, and commitments that affect employees, use the internal organizational culture vision as your aspirational reference point.

CHOCOLATE

Sophi Tranchell,
Divine Chocolate—
United Kingdom

Q: Why did you decide to become a B Corp?

A: Divine prides itself on doing business differently, and we are committed to our responsibility to people and planet in the way we operate. B Corp certification is an important third-party validation of our business practices, not only reflecting our total commitment to fair trade and cooperative values but also demonstrating those values running right through the company. It is our assurance to consumers that they can feel as confident about the way we run our business as they do about the benefits our products deliver to farmers around the globe.

Q: What business benefits do you directly attribute to your B Corp certification?

A: The opportunity to collaborate with the B Corp community both in the UK and U.S. has been the biggest benefit so far. It has helped us to drive brand reach and engagement in partnership with organizations that share the same values that we do. In the U.S., we also found that distributors championed Divine because of our B Corp certification, which in turn enabled us to gain new trade listings.

Q: What has your company done to help build a more inclusive economy?

A: Divine has been working hard to build a more inclusive economy since we were established in 1998. As the only Fairtrade chocolate company owned by its own suppliers, Divine has a mission to ensure farmers receive a greater share of the wealth they are creating and a stronger voice in the cocoa industry.

✓ **Train employees on your social and/or environmental mission.**

Why Is This Practice Rewarded?

Providing formal training about your social and/or environmental mission can help motivate and engage your employees by connecting them to the purpose behind your corporate objectives.

> *The number one thing we do to encourage employee engagement is take teammates on a trip to the rain forest to be a part of harvest in an Indigenous community. About half of our people have been there, and several of our teammates are based full time in Argentina or Paraguay. This really keeps everyone connected to the mission and vision and continues to inspire positivity across the company.*
>
> Chris Mann, Guayaki—USA

How Can You Implement This at Your Company?

Start by explaining your company's social and environmental goals to all new hires. Embed these goals in the employee handbook. Next, create training for all employees on your social mission. Ask one of your long-term employees, board members, or investors to give a presentation about how your company's mission aims to solve social or environmental challenges. For example, King Arthur Flour hosts ESOP 101, which explains how employee ownership addresses financial inequality, why King Arthur Flour is employee-owned, and how employees can become eligible to participate in the employee stock ownership plan.

One of the best ways to connect your employees to your values is to give them firsthand experience. For example, United By Blue's mission is to raise awareness about plastic pollution in the ocean. Although its core business is selling clothing made from recycled ocean plastics, the company also organizes river and beach cleanups that give employees a personal connection to the problem of plastic waste. All employees at United By Blue are encouraged to either attend or lead a cleanup as a step toward better understanding of the company's mission.

✓ **Evaluate employees and management on their performance with regard to the company's social and environmental targets. Consider tying social and environmental performance to bonuses or other rewards.**

Why Is This Practice Rewarded?

Are your employees and managers evaluated using written, predetermined social and environmental goals? If not, consider integrating these into your annual performance reviews. Creating accountability (and more incentives) for meeting social and environmental goals can increase employee engagement with your sustainability initiatives.

How Can You Implement This at Your Company?

Have a conversation with your employees about their performance reviews. Tell them why you are considering specific social and environmental goals and how this aligns with your company's values. Explaining the purpose behind the proposed changes, and allowing your employees to have a say in the process, will be much more effective than forced compliance.

One of the best ways to generate employee sustainability targets is to take the B Impact Assessment. This can help spark a wide variety of ideas, such as turning off lights that are not in use, biking to work at least once a week, organizing a carpool group, or recycling/composting whenever possible.

managers—accountable for inclusive behavior and cultural competency helps communicate that your workplace is one where bias, discrimination, and harassment are actively discouraged. Organizational leaders cannot tell people what to believe but they can dictate what is acceptable and unacceptable behavior. When behavior affects their paycheck, employees are highly incentivized to engage and perform in this area. Just be certain to define culturally competent behavior and to provide training and information so that people know exactly what is expected.

✓ **Solicit from your external stakeholders (customers, community members, suppliers, or nonprofit organizations) feedback about your company's social and environmental performance.**

Why Is This Practice Rewarded?

Businesses benefit from having a formal, structured process to solicit from its stakeholders feedback about the company's social and environmental impact. Stakeholders often are greatly affected by a company's decisions but usually have no say in the decision-making process. General customer satisfaction or product feedback, while important on its own, is not rewarded in this context.

How Can You Implement This at Your Company?

One of the best ways to generate new ideas about improving your performance is to ask the people who engage with your company on a regular basis. For example, try creating a specific social and environmental feedback section on your website, sending out an online survey, or creating a contest and giving out prizes. Start with your top five suppliers and/or your best customers. Use their feedback to refine and improve your practices.

DR. JANA'S TIPS: Be thoughtful about who is not in the room and which stakeholders may be overlooked. Are particular demographics being omitted deliberately? Do you want more diverse stakeholders? Can you find out why you don't have the diversity of stakeholders you seek? If you do have a broad representation of stakeholders, be certain to solicit their feedback on the strengths of your performance and opportunities for improvement.

✓ **Maintain a board of directors, advisory board, or other governing body that includes women, people of color, LGBTQ individuals, and other underrepresented individuals, as well as nonexecutive employees, community members, and environmental experts, and that reviews the company's social and environmental performance.**

Why Is This Practice Rewarded?

This question rewards companies that have a governing body that, in addition to reviewing sales and operations, also audits financials, oversees executive compensation, and reviews the company's social and environmental performance. In addition, governing bodies that include employees (that is, nonexecutive management), community members, and/or environmental experts also are rewarded, because their insights and expertise can help ensure that the company makes decisions that benefit all of its stakeholders.

> We have defined, in our bylaws, who shall make up our board of directors. It includes the following: at least one frontline employee; at least one supervisory-level employee; 50 percent of the board must be comprised of members that are not a shareholder or employee of the corporation and must have community and/or environmental expertise; at least 50 percent of the board must be comprised of people of color, women, LGBTQ, or individuals from underserved communities; at least one board member must be a representative of one of the corporation's customers; and at least one board member must be low-income.

Jennifer Coombs, Facilities Management Services—USA

Research shows that companies with more gender and racial diversity on their board of directors experience better financial performance, even when controlling for size, industry, and corporate governance structure. A study of Fortune 500 companies in 2009 showed that companies with the highest level of gender diversity on their boards experienced a 42 percent greater return on sales and a 53 percent higher return on equity compared with their peers.[35]

How Can You Implement This at Your Company?

Your governing body, whether you choose a formal board of directors or a more informal advisory body, will be much more likely to work well if it is composed of the right people. Members should be able to bring a new level of expertise, perspective, and value, adding a different dimension to decision making that complements the strengths of current board members, executives, and the company as a whole.

When choosing prospective board members, consider the strengths and weaknesses of your current leadership, the current and future needs of your organization, key stakeholder groups, and the business experience that prospective board members will require to be able to provide meaningful advice and guidance. Here are some steps you can take to start the process.

- Establish a plan and goal for diversifying your board. Avoid tokenism by ensuring you have more than one woman and/or person from an underrepresented group on the board.

- Make sure your job descriptions are inclusive in language and culture, attractive to a diverse pool of candidates (in terms of hours needed, growth opportunities, benefits, and so on) and focused on the skills and effort needed rather than on pedigree in education, networks, or other background that may unintentionally limit you to a homogenous pool of candidates.

- Widen your network to ensure you're interviewing highly skilled, diverse board candidates. Interview more than one underrepresented candidate for a position.

- Invest in orientation and mentoring for new directors and appoint new board members to committees that are consistent with their expertise.

Example: RSF Social Finance

RSF is a financial services agency dedicated to revolutionizing how we relate to money. Starting in 2009, RSF began hosting periodic gatherings to create greater transparency and connection between investors and borrowers in their social enterprise loan program. The theme of these meetings was interest rates—how much their investors earn and the interest that borrowers must pay on their loans. These meetings are now part of a quarterly process for determining a customized interest rate termed RSF Prime.

Their three stakeholder groups—investors, borrowers, and RSF staff—contribute their insight to assist RSF in setting a price that meets the needs of everyone. The meetings are an opportunity to learn about one another, to discuss what rates will best meet the needs of all stakeholders, and to make recommendations for raising or lowering the interest rate. RSF believes this methodology fits better with its mission to create financial relationships that are direct, transparent, and personal.

DR. JANA'S TIPS: As a person who is black, gender-nonconforming, pansexual, and suffers from depression and anxiety (an invisible disability that is discounted in society), I am often asked to participate on nonprofit boards of directors. I have spoken with minority friends and peers who are also tapped frequently for board service. I invite you to look beyond the limits of the visible, high-profile minority members of your community for board representation. These people often are overcommitted and less likely to engage as much as other folks, who would welcome the opportunity. Find passionate, talented people from representative demographics who may not have served on boards yet, people with connections to your mission but not necessarily with deep pockets. Some boards have seen successful diversification when they waived the board financial contribution requirement to make space for less affluent but more diverse members whose contributions are valuable without being monetary.

✓ **Produce an external annual report detailing your mission-related performance.**

Example: Tony's Chocolonely

Tony's Chocolonely, a chocolate company based in the Netherlands, produces an annual report on its social and environmental impact. Tony's asks its stakeholders (either in person or via a questionnaire) what subjects they would like the company to focus on each year. The company compares these responses with the subjects that the Tony's management team identified as important for the future of the company. From its 2015 report, Tony's learned that information about its workforce was not as interesting to external stakeholders. Tony's also learned that its environmental impact and the health impact of its products are issues that the company needs to focus on going forward. The company adjusted the content of its impact report to better account for the stakeholder feedback received.

Why Is This Practice Rewarded?

Sharing your mission-related performance with the public can help build consumer and local community trust. Producing an annual report is one of many ways to help show that your company is making progress toward its mission.

The process of creating an annual report can be very beneficial for your company. Some companies find that the process of compiling the information helps them uncover social and environmental risks, inefficiencies, and opportunities that otherwise would have gone unnoticed. This process also can be a helpful means of building consensus and internal accountability systems to better track your company's performance over time.

How Can You Implement This at Your Company?

If your company has never produced a mission-related report, the following are a few questions to consider:

- Do you have clear descriptions of your mission-related activities?
- Have you identified the positive and negative effects of your company's operations on society and the environment?
- Can you prepare quantifiable targets and results related to your mission (for instance, pounds of carbon offset)?
- Can you report with consistent variables of measurement, which will allow comparisons to previous years or other businesses?
- Have you solicited feedback from your various stakeholder groups to help determine which information to report?
- Is there third-party validation of the contents of your report?

If you would like a comprehensive, straightforward, and free tool to help you create a mission-related report, we encourage you to benchmark your company's performance by using the B Impact Assessment.

DR. JANA'S TIPS: Consider including your diversity, equity, and inclusion goals in your report. As B Corps, we should hold ourselves to higher standards, including in challenging spaces. Even if your diversity numbers don't look great, you have to start somewhere. Transparency shows that you are not hiding anything, and a visible commitment gives you something to aspire to and communicates that DEI is important and that you are trying.

✓ **Legally institutionalize your mission in your corporate governing documents.**

Why Is This Practice Rewarded?

If your company is good for workers, good for communities, and good for the environment, then it is important that your company's mission is protected for the long term. One of the best ways to protect your mission is to embed your company's core social and environmental values in your corporate governing documents—the legal DNA of your business. By elevating your values to the status of law, your company will be able to maintain its mission through changes in management and ownership. This practice is rewarded because the consideration of stakeholder interests in corporate decision making is a simple yet radical shift in the evolution of capitalism. For an interesting case study about how this can play out in real life, see the story about Whole Foods Market in the "Protecting a Company's Mission for the Long Term" section in part 2 of this book.

> *I hope that five years from now, ten years from now, we'll look back and say that B Corps were the start of the revolution. The existing paradigm isn't working anymore. This is the future.*

> Yvon Chouinard, Patagonia—USA

How Can You Implement This at Your Company?

The process of institutionalizing stakeholder interests in your governing documents is dependent on your location (the state or country in which your company is incorporated) and your existing legal structure. Remember that your place of incorporation can be different from where you operate. For example, in the United States, many companies are incorporated in Delaware but operate out of a different home state.

You'll be able to better understand the current laws governing your legal entity type in your jurisdiction with support from legal counsel. Because this varies around the world, some companies may already have mission-aligned governance incorporated into their structure, some may be able to amend their governing documents to include stakeholder consideration, and some may not have a current path to achieve mission-aligned governance without legislative changes or unless they change their company's legal structure. Appendix A of this book contains information about the differences between Certified B Corporations and benefit corporations.[36]

DR. JANA'S TIPS: Consider including an aspirational diversity, equity, and inclusion vision in your corporate governing documents. Organizations often develop missions that are entirely externally focused. To balance this, one best practice is to define the inclusive employee experience that you want people to have at your company. Rather than leaving organizational culture to chance, why not define it proactively and allow that vision to help shape future decisions? If the diversity vision is in the governing documents, there is no question about whether DEI is an organizational priority. This speaks volumes to current and future employees and is even more powerful if followed up with demonstrable and measurable action.

Quick Assessment of Customer Impact

Want to get a quick idea of how good your company is for customers? Take the following twelve-item Quick Assessment to measure your performance over the past year. You can add up your total at the bottom for a rough idea of how you might score on the Customers section of the B Impact Assessment.

Check the box if you and/or your company . . .

☐ cover your product or service with a written consumer warranty and/or client protection policy.

☐ have third-party certification of the quality of your products or services, which may include process certifications such as ISO 9000 or industry-specific quality accreditations.

☐ ensure that significant suppliers are subjected to regular quality assurance reviews or audits.

☐ have a tracking system in place to manage quality assurance issues.

☐ have a publicly known mechanism through which customers can provide product feedback, ask questions, or file complaints.

☐ measure customer satisfaction via a Net Promoter Score or other methodology.

☐ share customer satisfaction scores publicly.

☐ create specific increase targets for customer satisfaction.

- [ ] have a formal program to incorporate customer testing and feedback into product or service design.

- [ ] measure, manage, and reduce the potential negative outcomes your product or service may unintentionally create for customers.

- [ ] have a formal, publicly available policy on data privacy.

- [ ] make all customers aware of any data that your company collects, the length of time that data is preserved, how it is used, and whether it is shared with other public or private entities.

_____ **Total**

Give yourself one point for each affirmative response.

If you scored from zero to 3, you will have some work do to earn B Corp certification. Alternatively, you can make up ground with an outstanding performance in the other areas.

If you scored from 4 to 6, you are a good candidate for B Corp certification, assuming you perform similarly well on the other sections.

If you scored from 7 to 12, fantastic work! You are likely well on your way to getting the score you need for B Corp certification.

Corey Lien,
DOMI Earth—Taiwan

Q: Why did you decide to become a B Corp?

A: From the very beginning, we staked DOMI's success on impact. We decided that, even if we started making money and building a financially sustainable business, we wouldn't be satisfied unless we were also making significant, measurable progress toward environmental goals at scale. Because we focus on priorities like reducing greenhouse gas emissions, cutting energy consumption, and building community resilience to climate change, we knew that we needed to coordinate a lot of people. The B Corp movement was almost purpose-built for this kind of collaboration. So, in many ways, pursuing certification was a natural step in building a business with an environmental mission at its core.

Q: What was your biggest surprise about becoming a B Corp?

A: Hands down, the biggest surprise has been the community. When I interact with other B Corp founders and leaders, we spend a lot more time talking about our impact than we do about business deals. This builds a lot of trust, which ultimately leads to more business relationships, even with those outside the B Corp community. It also pushes us to do more, to compete with each other on impact, and to show up when our B "co-conspirators" ask for support. B Corp is a mind-set shift from "How can I get the advantage over you?" to "How do we combine and amplify our impact?" I believe the first model is soon to dry up and that there is an incredible amount of untapped value in the latter.

Customers

The Customers section is a relatively recent addition to the B Impact Assessment. B Lab added this section because excellent customer service, cultivating long-term customer relationships, and offering quality products and services not only is a core component of a company's strategy but also is one of the primary ways for a business to create value and positive impact. To help you on your journey, we will highlight some of these topics, discuss why they are important, explain why they are rewarded on the assessment, and offer tips for implementing these practices in your company.

✓ **Cover your product or service with a written consumer warranty and/or client protection policy.**

Why Is This Practice Rewarded?

When customers buy products or services, they want to be reassured that they're making the best decision possible. They need to know that what they spend their money on will last and, if it does not, that they can reach out to the company for support. Warranties are beneficial to both customers and business owners because they set expectations, protect both parties, and can encourage repeat sales.

How Can You Implement This at Your Company?

The following are some tips and guidelines for composing an effective warranty:

- Follow express rules and regulations.
- Clarify what the warranty covers.
- State the length of time that the product is covered.
- Give customers the option to extend.
- Consider assigning a specific person and/or creating a department to handle warranty concerns.

Service companies also can offer a warranty. For example, LIFT Economy uses "value-based invoicing" with clients. All consulting proposals include the following language:

> LIFT Economy is unique in how we bill our clients. We do not submit our invoice until the end of each month that we work. When you receive the invoice, you will be encouraged to adjust the billed amount (down or up) based on the value you feel you received. This means that we have to prove our value to you on a month-to-month basis—and you get to decide if it was worth it.

In other words, if a client feels that LIFT Economy has not provided sufficient value during the preceding month, the client can reduce the amount they pay—even reducing it to zero. This keeps the worker-owners at LIFT Economy very client-focused. It also shortens the sales cycle because there is no risk for prospective clients to try working with LIFT Economy for at least one month.

It should be noted that Ryan Honeyman has had only three invoices adjusted over the past several years. Each of these adjustments resulted in the client paying Ryan *more*, by doubling the amount of the invoice. All of the other partners at LIFT Economy have had similar results while working with more than 150 social enterprises over the past ten years.

✓ **Ensure that significant suppliers are subjected to regular quality assurance reviews or audits. Implement a tracking system to manage quality assurance issues.**

Why Is This Practice Rewarded?

A large number of quality incidents are related to supplier quality issues. These issues can have substantial impact on customers and on the bottom line of a company. As a result, companies are increasingly focusing on understanding these challenges and addressing them with a proactive and collaborative approach toward supplier quality management.

How Can You Implement This at Your Company?

To identify the key drivers of quality problems, McKinsey & Company examined more than forty recent quality incidents across eight different industry sectors. McKinsey's research identified three root causes: lack of collaboration in the design phase, lack of a robust quality system or the right key performance indicators, and lack of capabilities in manufacturing. McKinsey argues that each of these issues could have been avoided if the customers had possessed a more comprehensive understanding of the suppliers' knowledge, quality assurance processes, and manufacturing capabilities.[37]

Perhaps the best way to ensure quality is to seek out suppliers that are third-party certified. Third-party certification means that an independent organization has reviewed the manufacturing process of a product and has independently determined that the final product complies with specific standards for quality. This review typically includes a comprehensive audit of many different layers of an organization.

The industry standard for quality certification is ISO 9000. The ISO 9000 standards are based on seven quality management principles that senior management can apply for organizational improvement. These seven principles include customer focus, leadership, engagement of people, process approach, improvement, evidence-based decision making, and relationship management. To learn more about ISO 9000, visit the International Organization for Standardization website.[38]

✓ **Create a publicly known mechanism through which customers can provide product feedback, ask questions, or file complaints. Measure customer satisfaction via a Net Promoter Score or other methodology and share these scores publicly. Create specific increase targets for customer satisfaction.**

Why Is This Practice Rewarded?

All business leaders know that they will be more successful if their customers are happier. But how do you keep your customers happy? How do you know what your customers like or dislike about your product? Asking for customer feedback can provide valuable insight into your business and your products. It can help you learn what your customers like and do not like, make customers feel important and involved, and help you constantly improve your products and/or services.

How Can You Implement This at Your Company?

An easy way to make progress on this goal is to ensure that your company has a public-facing online review page on a site like Yelp, Google, or Facebook. You should ensure that your company's website has links directly to your online review page so that customers know where to find it.

If you are looking for a more specialized means of understanding your brand's strength, Net Promoter Score is a popular methodology. NPS is designed to measure customer satisfaction and loyalty with one question: "How likely is it that you would recommend our organization to a friend or colleague?" Customers are asked to provide their answer on a scale of zero to 10 (with zero being "extremely unlikely" and 10 being "extremely likely"). The results are then broken into three categories:

- **0 to 6: Detractors.** These are unhappy customers who can hurt your brand through negative word of mouth.
- **7 or 8: Passives.** These are satisfied but indifferent customers who could be swayed by the competition.
- **9 or 10: Promoters.** These are loyal customers who will keep buying and will refer others.

The NPS system is popular because it goes beyond a simple measurement of customer satisfaction. It helps you identify whether people are promoting your business. Although there are some criticisms of NPS, many studies have shown that the NPS system does correlate with business growth. Studies by the *Harvard Business Review*, Forrester, and Satmetrix have found that an improved Net Promoter Score can result in increased income and improved customer retention. Another benefit is that NPS allows you to benchmark your company's results against others in your industry. For those who are interested in giving it a try, SurveyMonkey offers a free Net Promoter Score survey template that you can use with your customers and clients.[39]

DR. JANA'S TIPS: A publicly known mechanism creates an inclusive experience for customers to engage with your brand and provide valuable feedback. This is an important access point for members of marginalized groups who do not always feel as if their voice matters. Customers appreciate being able to help improve products and services and to have their concerns addressed when something goes wrong. This helps people feel valued, regardless of demographic identity. Also be sure to solicit alternative or innovative uses for your products, as customers are often identifying new markets well in advance of formal research and development. Your users are key to your growth.

✓ **Create a formal program to incorporate customer testing and feedback into product or service design.**

Why Is This Practice Rewarded?

Continually incorporating customers' opinions into the initial design, testing, and rollout phases can lead to products or services that more closely match customer needs. In turn, this can help with customer retention, create stronger brand loyalty, and increase engagement with your brand.

How Can You Implement This at Your Company?

Launching a new initiative—whether it is a start-up business or a new project within an existing company—has traditionally been a hit-or-miss proposition. According to the traditional formula, you write an extensive plan, pitch it to key stakeholders, assemble a team, introduce the new product or service, and start trying to find customers. The problem is that most start-ups, products, and services are not successful.

The "lean" start-up favors experimentation over elaborate planning, customer feedback over intuition, and iterative design. The lean start-up methodology seeks to eliminate wasteful practices during the product development phase so that start-ups can have a better overall chance of success. Customer feedback during product development is integral to the lean start-up process and ensures that the producer does not invest time in designing features or services that consumers do not want. For more on this subject, the book *The Lean Startup: How Today's Entrepreneurs Use Continuous Innovation to Create Radically Successful Businesses*, by Eric Ries, is essential reading.

DR. JANA'S TIPS: This practice gives customers a voice and a role in shaping your products and services. Ensure that your process includes diverse pools of people so that you can access multiple perspectives and market opportunities.

✓ **Measure, manage, and reduce the potential negative outcomes your product or service may unintentionally create for customers.**

Why Is This Practice Rewarded?

The B Impact Assessment rewards companies whose products and/or services create a positive impact on society and the environment. Some businesses, however, while striving to create a positive impact, can unintentionally create negative social or environmental outcomes for their stakeholders. These unintended outcomes are called second-order effects. Managing for potential negative outcomes encourages businesses to think more holistically about the second-order effects of their products and or services.

For example, a solar installation company may help shift the economy away from fossil fuels to clean energy. However, the solar panels might be manufactured by a supplier that dumps hazardous chemicals into a nearby river. The solar installation company would be rewarded if it considered these second-order effects and worked with its suppliers to minimize negative environmental impacts. A different example might be that of a home builder that promotes the densification of urban areas to reduce housing sprawl, promote better land use, and reduce climate emissions. The unintended downside of this strategy, however, might be that historically marginalized groups, especially low-income individuals and people of color, are priced out of rapidly gentrifying cities. The home builder would be rewarded on the assessment when it works with affected communities in its area to reduce these unintended negative outcomes.

How Can You Implement This at Your Company?

Consider the multiple layers of impact your product or service has on customers. In particular, consider how the second-order effects of your product or service may affect women, people of color, immigrants, formerly incarcerated individuals, low-income individuals, Indigenous peoples, and other historically marginalized communities. Here are some questions you can ask to help you think about unintended negative outcomes:

- What are the probable negative outcomes of a new product or service you are considering?
- What are the probable consequences of those consequences?
- What can you do to minimize the risks of those unintended negative impacts?
- What can you do to ensure that historically disadvantaged groups are not negatively affected by your product or service?
- Who do you need to involve in the discussion early to ensure that a diverse group of stakeholders can give you their thoughts, feedback, and advice on your plans?

Jeff Ward,
Animikii—Canada

Q: Why did you decide to become a B Corp?

A: I decided to become a B Corp on a recommendation from a friend who hinted that my business of twelve years probably already operated with many principles found in B Corps. As a learning experience, I ventured into the B Corp world and social innovation world to find that our little Indigenous tech company operated like a "social enterprise," though I never used that language to describe us.

Q: What business benefits do you directly attribute to your B Corp certification?

A: It has given me the language to explain to the broader business community how Indigenous entrepreneurs and businesses already commonly operate. It has connected the work we do and our story to the B Corp community, and we've been received with open arms.

Q: If you could change one thing about the B Corp movement, what would it be?

A: I would add universal questions and examples into the B Impact Assessment that specifically called out and measured impact on the local Indigenous communities in which B Corps operate.

Q: What was your biggest surprise about becoming a B Corp?

A: I was surprised at the amount of work that goes into becoming certified. I now know, when I see that B Corp logo, how much work went into doing that, and maintaining it. But after certification, I was pleasantly surprised to learn from and meet other like-minded and passionate individuals who are also using business as a force for good.

DR. JANA'S TIPS: Be careful not to overlook this aspect. We can do good in the world without further marginalizing vulnerable populations. It can take longer, and be more expensive, to consult with and protect those who do not have the resources to successfully defend their own interests (including health and safety). However, if we are here to use business as a force for good, can we really afford to turn a blind eye to the needs of the less fortunate? Can we be proud of ourselves and the B Economy if we perpetuate injustice by exploiting the same perverse mechanisms that created and continue to reinforce wealth and income inequality?

✓ **Create a formal, publicly available data and privacy policy. Ensure that all customers are aware of any information that your company collects, the length of time that it is preserved, how it is used, and whether it is shared with other public or private entities.**

Why Is This Practice Rewarded?

Customer information must be protected for the benefit of your brand, for your bottom line, and most importantly, for the privacy of your customers. According to one estimate from IBM, the average out-of-pocket cost of security breaches has now climbed to $4 million per incident—up nearly 30 percent in only a few years.[40]

How Can You Implement This at Your Company?
Business owners should consider the following five questions to get a better assessment of their responsibilities with respect to protecting customer data:

- What personal customer information does your business have?
- Do you have more private data than you need?
- Is your sensitive data properly secured?
- Have you properly disposed of customer data that is no longer needed?
- Do you have a data security response plan in place?

4

The Quick Start Guide

Welcome to the six-step Quick Start Guide. This section is designed both for businesses that want to become Certified B Corporations and for those that are unsure about certification but want a straightforward, step-by-step road map to help them measure, compare, and improve their social and environmental performance.

If you are unsure about whether B Corp certification is right for you, feel free to do as much (or as little) of the following section as you wish. This six-step guide can be seen as an informal resource to help you plan and implement improvements to your business. Those who wish to become certified should follow the same six-step guide, and there are a few extra tasks you will need to complete to meet the minimum requirements. These extra steps are marked "B Corps only" in each segment.

> *Keep your cool, work with the folks from B Lab, and don't panic or fret. B Corp certification is more of a journey-based process than a destination-based reward.*

> Daniel Andrade, BILD—Bolivia

Just as "Dr. Jana's Tips" on diversity, equity, and inclusion are included throughout the book, this section includes "Ryan's Tips" on how to manage the B Impact Assessment and the B Corp certification process quickly and effectively.

Whether you are seeking B Corp certification or not, the size and complexity of your company will affect how quickly you can move through the following section. We have found that you will have the best chance of successfully completing this process if:

- you have the ability to see that "the perfect is the enemy of the good." If you try to be perfect on the B Impact Assessment, you run the risk of getting bogged down and never finishing. Aim for good enough and continue to improve your score in the future.

- you or someone else in your company "owns" the project. If many people are working on a project, it often means that no one is actually responsible for moving it forward. Make sure that someone (whether it is you, an external consultant, or another employee) has taken ownership of the project and will dedicate the time and energy necessary to see it through to completion.
- you have access to financial, worker, supplier, community, and environmental data. If you don't personally have access to this data, you need access to the people who are responsible for this data (e.g., the facility manager for energy usage or the human resources manager for employee metrics).
- you proactively engage with and provide value to the B Corp community upon completion of B Corp certification. Over the past few years, a few companies have certified as B Corps and then immediately started to pitch their products and services to a large number of B Corps. This is not a good approach. Although the community welcomes all new Certified B Corporations, we also want to build long-term relationships with you that are based on mutual respect and support. Try giving selflessly to the community. You may be surprised at how much value you receive in return.

Step 1: Get a Baseline

Objective: The objective during step 1 is to use the B Impact Assessment to establish a quick baseline of your company's overall social and environmental performance and to create momentum before engaging others in the process.

End result: A rough B Impact Report for your company.

✓ **Create your B Impact Assessment account.** Create your free account online at bimpactassessment.net. As you register, you will be asked questions about your company's size, industry, and location in order to generate a version of the assessment that is tailored to fit your business. For example, a marketing company with six employees will see different questions than a furniture manufacturer with six thousand employees.

✓ **Start the Quick Impact Assessment.** The first thing you will encounter is the Quick Impact Assessment. This is an abridged version of the assessment that provides a snapshot of your social and environmental impact. The goal is to give you a simple look at the practices your company already excels at and the practices you could improve upon. This can be a very useful starting point. If you want to get a numerical score (between zero and 200 points), you will need to move to the next stage.

João Paulo Ferreira,
Natura—Brazil

Q: Why did you decide to become a B Corp?

A: At the end of 2013, we were studying Natura's 2020/2050 sustainability vision and we started to evaluate the strategic evolution of sustainability as a whole. For this study, we sought out trends in all areas of social, environmental, and economic innovation. The B Corp movement emerged during our research as a possible formula for our business's evolution. While this was happening, we were sought out by the B Movement, and that is how our paths converged. We saw an opportunity to reaffirm Natura's DNA in line with this movement's purpose—to integrate financial results with the generation of social and environmental results—thus redefining the concept of business success.

Q: What business benefits do you directly attribute to your B Corp certification?

A: B Corp certification is a stimulus for Natura to constantly strive to be a better company for the world. This is because the certification is renewed every three years, driving us to constantly update our strategy. In 2017, Natura scored 120 points, while the average for other B Corp companies in the industrial sector is 105. In addition, as soon as Natura joined the B Corp movement, we found that other companies started wanting to use us as a benchmark. Companies see Natura as a role model. They want to know what we have done differently in order to achieve B Corp certification.

✓ **Convert to the full B Impact Assessment.** Once you have answered all of the questions in the Quick Impact Assessment, you will be eligible to convert your assessment to the full version. All of your answers from the Quick Impact Assessment will be carried over. As you move through the full version of the assessment, remember to estimate your answers and to avoid spending more than a minute or two on any particular question. The goal is to get a rough baseline of your practices.

RYAN'S TIPS: If you are unsure about how to answer a particular question, flag it and revisit it later. Don't dig up specific data or e-mail or call anyone until you have finished your initial pass through. At the end of the assessment, you can run a "revisit report" that enables you to see all of the questions you guessed on, estimated, or didn't know how to answer. Use this report to create a single, comprehensive e-mail for each person from whom you need information (such as your accountant, human resources person, or facilities manager). This approach is a much more effective use of everyone's time and energy.

✓ **Review your preliminary score.** At the end of your first pass through the full assessment, you will receive a baseline B Impact Report that gives you a holistic look at your company's overall social and environmental performance. This report will also contain benchmarks to allow you to compare your performance to more than fifty thousand other businesses that have completed the assessment.

✓ **Did you score 20 to 40?** Don't get too discouraged about a low initial score. Some companies that started with a score in this range have made it all the way to B Corp certification (scoring above 80 points) with focused and consistent effort over time.

✓ **Did you score 40 to 60?** An overall B Impact Score of 40 to 60 is average. This means that you've got a solid foundation on which to build. The fun part will be working with your colleagues to determine which impact areas (Governance, Workers, Community, Environment, and/or Customers) you want to improve.

✓ **Did you score 60 to 80?** If you received an overall B Impact Score of 60 or higher, nice work! It sounds like your company has already adopted quite a few socially and environmentally responsible practices. From here, your goal will be to help mobilize your team to improve your performance in the areas that matter most to you and your company.

✓ **Did you score 80 or higher?** If you received an overall B Impact Score of 80 or higher, congratulations! Eighty is the minimum score necessary for B Corp certification. If you are interested, we highly recommend that you consider submitting your assessment to B Lab for verification and pursuing B Corp certification to give your company the recognition it deserves.

✓ **Regardless of your initial overall score, remember that this is a journey of continuous improvement.** Are there areas you and others in your company should be proud of? Are there areas you would like to work on? This will give you a few things to think about as you move forward into step 2.

Step 2: Engage Your Team

Objective: Identify coworkers who may be interested in helping you use your business as a force for good. During this part of the process you will have a chance to get different people involved and to get help answering any questions that you marked "revisit."

End result: An informal working group to help you update your B Impact Report with more accurate information.

✓ Set up a meeting with key internal stakeholders. The first step to securing early buy-in and building project momentum is to organize a meeting with the key people in your company. The invite list for this meeting might include, for example, your CEO, CFO, COO, sustainability director, marketing director, human resources manager, or building manager. If you are in the manufacturing or wholesale sectors, you may wish to include key individuals from the product design, sourcing, and supply chain divisions. You want the decision makers in the room so you can bring everyone up to speed. This will help you build momentum as the project moves forward. Be mindful about including diverse perspectives, such as tenure, age, race, gender, ability, seniority, and more. Different perspectives will help you brainstorm more inclusive solutions.

✓ **Explain the objectives and benefits.** Explain what you are trying to achieve, what you think success would look like, and how this project will benefit the company. For example, you could say, "There is a big opportunity to use our business as a force for good, and we need your help figuring out how to drive our company toward this vision." It can help to tailor your presentation based on who is attending the meeting, because certain objectives, metrics of success, and benefits will appeal to particular executives. For example:

- the CEO wants to attract and retain diverse talent;
- the CFO wants to attract investors and/or save money;
- human resources wants to motivate and engage employees;
- the marketing team may want to generate press, join a national ad campaign, or benefit from a trusted third-party standard;
- the sales team wants to increase consumer trust and/or create partnerships with other mission-aligned businesses;
- operations managers want to save money through operational efficiency;
- sustainability managers want to benchmark performance, share best practices, or earn recognition; and
- everyone wants a network with high-performing peers.

✓ **Share the assessment process and results.** Explain that you have already kick-started your company's journey by completing a baseline and generating a preliminary score. Share what you have learned through the B Impact Report, the best practice examples, and any relevant case studies. Invite a discussion about the opportunities for the company. What matters most to different individuals? What matters most to the team? What are the biggest strengths and weaknesses?

✓ **Identify a core project team.** Although there may be a wide variety of internal stakeholders at this meeting, you should try to identify a core project team that can help you dig into the details, create an improvement plan, and implement any changes. Be thoughtful about diversity and inclusion by considering people from different backgrounds and at various levels of the organization. This project team may or may not include your management team. Line managers, associates, interns, and even board members can be a huge support in helping to turn ideas into action. Be thoughtful about diversity and inclusion.

RYAN'S TIPS: When creating a project team, choose passion over seniority. For example, a highly motivated associate can be a more effective teammate than an uninspired CFO. Although you want senior-level buy-in, this does not mean that every senior executive needs to help with project execution. Also, try to create a project team that is diverse and inclusive. Include women, people of color, and other underrepresented groups and ensure that their voices are heard.

Once you have a team, try to be mindful about the informal power dynamics. Who is speaking up more than others? Who gets to decide which areas of the B Impact Assessment to focus on? If the company scored poorly on the diversity section of the assessment, will your team focus on that? There is not necessarily a "right" answer for every situation. The goal is to seek to include traditionally underrepresented voices and appropriately balance the power dynamics of the team.

✓ **Set clear next steps.** Set up a meeting with your core project team. The goal of this meeting will be to start moving forward with the data collection and implementation process.

✓ **Start discussing the B Corp legal framework (B Corps only).** Discuss with key board members, legal counsel, and investors why it is important to maintain the company's mission over the long term. Reference benefitcorp.net for information and resources about different legal options.

Step 3: Create a Plan

Objective: After you have identified your core project team, work with them to set a target B Impact Score and create an action plan with short-, medium-, and long-term goals. For example, if you started out with a score of 53, see whether you can implement enough practices to earn an additional ten points by the end of this Quick Start Guide.

End result: An action plan with specific people assigned to take the lead on each question, a target B Impact Score, and a rough timeline for completion.

✓ **Use the improvement tools.** Show your team the improvement report within the B Impact Assessment. This report contains any questions that you marked for improvement, alongside improvements that are suggested by B Lab.

✓ **Prioritize.** You can approach the process of improving your score in different ways. Initially, address easy practices that do not require a lot of work to implement. For example, tracking employee volunteer hours is much easier than making a legal conversion to a benefit corporation. Save the things that will require lots of time, energy, discussion, and senior-level approval for later in the process.

FAIRPHONE

Bas van Abel,
Fairphone—Netherlands

Q: Why did you decide to become a B Corp?

A: Becoming a B Corp shows our values to others and helps us connect with like-minded companies that have a social mission at the heart of their operations.

Q: What was the biggest challenge you had to overcome to certify as a B Corp?

A: Fairphone has a (perhaps unique) background of originally being an awareness-raising campaign that transformed into a company. It was not very difficult to certify, because we started out as a very different kind of business. Becoming a B Corp has always been in our DNA.

Q: What was your biggest surprise about becoming a B Corp?

A: How effective it is in explaining our mission to people. Certifications like B Corp are great in helping make others aware of your larger purpose. This is really important for a company that was founded on a social mission.

Q: What is your company doing to help build a more inclusive economy?

A: Fairphone is changing the electronics industry from the inside out. We are changing the way products are made and how people consume them by reconnecting people to their phones and the supply chains behind them. To enable ethical consumerism, people need to know more about their products. We are improving the supply chain step by step and are showing that there is a demand for more ethical products.

✓ **Delegate responsibility.** For example, your human resources manager might take the lead on figuring out how to implement a job-sharing program, and your COO might start gathering data on the environmental practices of your suppliers.

✓ **Consider hiring a B Corp consultant.** There is a growing community of B Corp consultants who can help you make progress on the B Impact Assessment. Reach out to Ryan and/or B Lab for recommendations about consultants who could help you.

Step 4: Implement

Objective: The objective during step 4 is for you and your team to dig in and start completing the items on your action plan.

End result: An increase in your B Impact Assessment score.

✓ **Gather data and research.** Depending on your action plan, this is where you start identifying the financial, worker, supplier, community, environmental, and customer data required to update your B Impact Assessment responses. If necessary, contact the people responsible for the data you need.

✓ **Create policies and procedures.** One of the best ways to earn points on the B Impact Assessment is to formalize your policies and procedures in writing. For example, your company can earn points by creating an environmental purchasing policy, a local purchasing policy, a community service policy, an employee handbook, a whistle-blowing policy, a code of ethics, a supplier code of conduct, or an external annual report that details your mission-related performance.

Step 5: Fine Tune

Objective: As your team is working through the action plan, keep track of your improvements by inserting your data into the B Impact Assessment. This will give you an updated score.

End result: A recalculated and refined B Impact Assessment score.

✓ **Ready to tackle bigger items?** Depending on the measures you have implemented, your score may have improved since your initial assessment results. Now is a good time to reconnect with the key internal stakeholders in your company, such as the people you invited to the summit during step 2. Update these key stakeholders on your progress so far and have a conversation about the remaining (and possibly bigger) action items on your list. If you have not done so already, have a discussion about whether your company is interested in becoming a Certified B Corporation.

✓ **Submit your assessment (B Corps only).** Are you all ready to move forward? Is your current score on the B Impact Assessment at least 80 points or higher? If so, go ahead and submit your assessment for review.

✓ **Schedule an assessment review (B Corps only).** After submitting your B Impact Assessment, B Lab's staff will be notified and will reach out to you to schedule an assessment review. In preparation for the review call, B Lab's staff will ask you to upload supporting documentation for six to ten randomly selected questions that were answered in the affirmative. For example, if you said you have an environmental purchasing policy, B Lab's staff may ask you to upload that policy to the B Impact Assessment for review. You will be sent instructions about how to upload these requested documents prior to your review call.

✓ **Complete the assessment review (B Corps only).** During this call, B Lab's staff will review each of your responses with you. The goal is to give you a better understanding of the intent behind each question and an idea of what it would take to implement that practice. Most businesses find that they make adjustments to their answers after they receive clarification from a B Lab staff member. Any representative of your company (whether an executive, an associate, or an intern) can complete this assessment review call.

✓ **Did your score remain above 80 points (B Corps only)?** After the phone review, did your score remain above 80 points? If so, the assessment will select an additional three to six heavily weighted questions and ask you to demonstrate detailed proof of those practices through more documentation. If your score dropped below 80, go back to the improvement report in the B Impact Assessment to identify practices that can raise your score. Your assessment reviewer at B Lab can give you basic recommendations to help you identify any low-hanging fruit. Alternatively, see step 3 for thoughts on hiring a B Corp consultant to help you finish your certification.

✓ **Make it official (B Corps only).** Once you get the final approval from your assessment reviewer, B Lab's staff will send you an electronic version of the B Corp terms and conditions and the B Corporation Declaration of Interdependence to sign. B Lab also will ask you to pay the applicable B Corp certification fee to complete your certification process. A link to current B Corp certification fees can be found at bcorporation.net.

RYAN'S TIPS: Remind your staff to save any notes they have on why and how they answered certain questions on the assessment. These notes will come in handy if your company decides to become a B Corporation and you are asked to produce evidence of your practices.

Step 6: Celebrate, and Next Steps

Objective: By this time, you will have made significant progress toward improving your social and environmental performance. If you have met the requirements to become a Certified B Corporation, congratulations on joining one of the most exciting and dynamic movements in business!

End result: Celebrate, and congratulate your team for taking this journey.

✓ **Publicize your accomplishments.** Use this opportunity to share your success widely. Write an article in your company newsletter about your journey, accomplishments, and long-term plan. Try convening a "lunch and learn" with your staff to share your progress and encourage other employees to get involved. You also can publicize your achievement on your website, in your newsletter, and on social media channels to engage external stakeholders.

✓ **Consider building a stronger foundation.** In the majority of U.S. states and several countries, including Italy and Colombia, the community of Certified B Corporations has helped pass legislation in support of a new corporate form called the benefit corporation. The benefit corporation gives entrepreneurs the freedom to consider shareholders, workers, suppliers, community, customers, and the environment when making decisions. This helps ensure that your social and environmental mission can better survive new management, new investors, or even new ownership. See appendix A for additional details on the difference between Certified B Corporations and benefit corporations. Note that other designations, such as limited liability company, limited liability partnership, low-profit limited liability company, and sole proprietor, also are open to structural changes that satisfy the legal requirement to become a Certified B Corporation. Go to bcorporation.net for details about your specific situation.

✓ **Focus on continual improvement.** Like many things in life, this is not a quick fix but a process of continual improvement. For example, can your team continue to meet on a recurring basis to identify improvements? What questions did you skip during this initial process that could increase your company's impact before recertification in three years? What other big-picture goals do you want to strive for? Clarify how you and your team will continue to work toward achieving your social and environmental goals. Establish performance targets, and perhaps incentives, for achieving those ideal outcomes.

✓ **Check out the B Hive (B Corps only).** A great next step for new Certified B Corporations is to visit the B Hive. The B Hive is a platform the B Corp community can use to connect, access resources, collaborate, share knowledge, and offer discounts to one another. Any employee of any B Corp can register for the B Hive and start exploring the platform. Visit bcorporation.net for specific instructions about how to access the B Hive.

RYAN'S TIPS: Want to get the most value out of your B Corp certification? I often tell folks, "Ask not what the B Corp movement can do for you, but what you can do for the B Corp movement." I strongly encourage you to approach the community with an abundance mind-set. Come to the annual B Corp Champions Retreat, attend a B Corp Leadership Development conference, participate in a B Local group, or participate in a diversity, equity, and inclusion Peer Exchange group. Get to know the community. In my experience, being proactive and providing value to the B Corp community will repay itself many times over. Sitting back and waiting for B Lab (or other B Corps) to shower you with appreciation, introductions, and new business development opportunities can lead to disappointment.

method.

Onnia Harris,
Method—USA

Q: What has been your experience working for a B Corp?

A: I love working for Method! Our company has great community engagement, social impact, a beautiful working environment, and an amazing culture. The Soapbox is my extended family away from home. I have met some wonderful people, and even my children feel a part of the Method family. My children have volunteered with me at some of the Method events, such as Earth Day and Family Day at the Soapbox (our LEED Platinum manufacturing facility on the South Side of Chicago).

Q: What are some of the benefits you have received working at your company?

A: I have been an employee for two years now and have grown a lot personally and professionally. For example, I got promoted to operations production lead after working here for only a year and a half. That is a big accomplishment for me—especially since I came in as a temporary associate with no factory experience or skills. In addition, we have a carpool program where we give out gas cards; "care days," where we get paid to volunteer in the community; and, most importantly, we have the Soapbox giveaway, where we give free product to our employees and contract staffers.

Q: Anything else you would like to add?

A: I love coming to a place where I can bring my whole self to work. I have worked a lot of different jobs, but I have finally found the place I will retire from.

CONCLUSION

What Does Success for the B Corp Movement Look Like?

In a short amount of time, the B Corporation movement has brought together a global community of innovative, passionate, and forward-thinking business leaders who are committed to meeting some of the world's greatest social and environmental challenges. The rapid growth of the B Corp community worldwide, the legislative success across multiple countries, with strong bipartisan approval, and an increasing number of companies measuring and managing their impact with the B Impact Assessment shows that the idea of harnessing the power of business to drive systemic change is widely appealing.

There has undoubtedly been progress, but what does success for the B Corp movement look like? Success, for example, is not necessarily rapid growth in the number of Certified B Corporations and benefit corporations. Even if there were

B THE CHANGE. Attendees at a B Corp event in Australia learn about using the power of business as a force for good.

hundreds of thousands of Certified B Corporations and benefit corporations, that figure would represent a tiny fraction of the total number of businesses worldwide.

A more valuable measurement of success would be a dramatic increase in the number of businesses that measure what matters (that is, social and environmental performance in addition to financial performance) by using credible whole-business benchmarking tools such as the B Impact Assessment. When businesses measure the effects of their operations on all of their stakeholders, compare themselves with their industry peers, and start to compete to be the best *for* the world rather than just the best *in* the world, we will be making progress toward a more equitable future.

In preparing the second edition of this book, we put out a call to the global B Corp community to respond to a hypothetical. We asked respondents to imagine that it is the year 2030 and that they are proud that the B Corp movement has reached its collective goals. "Looking back," we asked, "what exactly has changed? What goals were met? How will you be able to prove this success to others?" Here are a few of the responses to the question "What would success for the B Corp movement look like in 2030?"

> *B Corps have made gender inequality and discrimination a distant memory. More opportunities are available today for diverse and underrepresented individuals than ever before. The belief that "success is only real when it touches everyone" is commonplace.*
>
> Federica Maria Mauro, Nativa—Italy

> *The demographics of the B Corp community (in terms of race, gender, income, etc.) mirror the demographics of the different regions in which B Corps reside. In particular, the percentage of women and people of color who are leaders and owners of B Corps is proportionate to their actual representation in society.*
>
> Jay Coen Gilbert, B Lab—USA

> *Damaged ecosystems have been restored. The continued drawdown of carbon emissions is on track to reverse the negative impacts of climate change.*
>
> Alicja Wojewnik, Vitarock—Canada

The baseline for the "business as usual" economy has improved so much that "standard" companies can score 80 points on the B Impact Assessment.

Caroline Duell, All Good—USA

The B Corp logo is recognized by the majority of consumers and is sought after by business owners and managers.

Adrianne Chandra-Huff, Bodhi Surf + Yoga—Costa Rica

The cost of externalities is included in the price of goods. Customers are not willing to buy anything without a triple bottom line calculation of price.

Gabor Levai, Civil Support Public Benefit Limited—Hungary

B Corps are part of the standard teaching curricula for all high schools and colleges around the globe.

Ann Hoogenboom, KSV—USA

Businesses must measure their impact in order to be publicly listed on any stock exchange.

Mercedes Viola, 4D Content English—Uruguay

We have to stay humble. If we reach 2030 and think "Our work here is done," then we've missed out on something. At best, we can say "Look how far we've come" and "Look at how far we have yet to go."

Stacy Metzger, PV Squared Solar—USA

In other words, success includes B Corp ownership that is demographically representative of the world in which we live. Success includes an increase in the percentage of new businesses that incorporate stakeholder interests into their foundational documents. Success includes more businesses measuring the social and environmental performance of their supply chains, helping suppliers to increase their overall performance, and using this impact data to make future procurement decisions. Success includes an increase in economic opportunity for the most marginalized groups in all of our societies. Success includes an increase in the number of business school graduates who work for companies that measure what matters. Growth in any of these figures—regardless of the total number of Certified B Corporations—would mean that creating value for workers, communities, customers, and the environment, in addition to shareholders, is an idea that resonates with current and future entrepreneurs.

The Work Still Left to Be Done on Diversity, Equity, and Inclusion

Although B Corps have made a lot of progress, we know that our community still has a long way to go before achieving our collective goals. What can B Corps do differently to create a more inclusive economy? What needs to change? How can we be better? In conversations with different B Corp leaders over the past few years, we have gathered some ideas about ways our community can continue to improve on DEI.

B Corps and Activism

One of the guiding principles of the B Corp community is "We stand for something, not against anything." This principle has served the B Corp community well. This solutions-based approach has helped the B Corp community to focus on how we can do the most good through business.

However, our world is different from when the B Corp movement was founded, more than ten years ago. Perhaps it is time for the B Corp community to get more involved in activism. Ben & Jerry's outspoken support of Black Lives Matter, Seventh Generation's work on toxics reduction, and Patagonia's decision to sue the U.S. government over the elimination of protected land are examples that come to mind. Others in the B Corp community have advocated that we start to demand a seat at the table at the United Nations, at climate conferences, or at other major gatherings of leaders.

Of course, this approach has to be strategic. It is going to take a lot of discussion and careful thought within the B Corp community to come together around the things we want to stand against. However, we believe there could be a better balance between focusing on solutions and protesting injustice.

Dismantling White Supremacy

As we discussed in the introduction to this book, one of the biggest opportunities to contribute to a shared and durable prosperity is to better understand how the legacies of white supremacy and colonialism show up in us as individuals, in our organizations, in the B Corp movement, and in society more broadly. Although it is outside the scope of this book to delve deeply into the process of naming, disrupting, and dismantling white supremacy, helpful books on this topic include *White Fragility*, by Robin DiAngelo; *Decolonizing Wealth*, by Edgar Villanueva; and *Waking Up White*, by Debby Irving. If any white readers feel that they already "get it" and do not need to learn about white supremacy, Robin DiAngelo has a good statement on the topic:

> I believe that white progressives cause the most daily damage to people of color. I define a white progressive as any white person who thinks he or she is not racist, or is less racist, or in the "choir," or already "gets it." White progressives can be the most difficult for people of color because, to the degree that we think we have arrived, we will put our energy into making sure that others see us as having arrived. None of our energy will go into what we need to be doing for the rest of our lives: engaging in ongoing self-awareness, continuing education, relationship building, and actual antiracist practice. White progressives do indeed uphold and perpetrate racism, but our defensiveness and certitude make it virtually impossible to explain to us how we do so.[1]

Shifting the Needle in Communities We Serve

While we each chip away at the issues about which we are individually passionate, what could we accomplish if we worked together toward a more targeted goal? As Diana Marie Lee, founder of B Corp Sweet Livity stated, "If all of the B Corps worldwide focused some of their energy on the same challenge for a given period of time, we could affect a monumental shift in the disparity, inequities, and injustices we are pledged to correct. For example, imagine the impact if every B Corp focused on addressing homelessness for one year. This could really demonstrate the power of our community."

Globally Inclusive Dialogue

Groups of people are marginalized all over the world. How is DEI being talked about in other countries? Is the global community creating space for groups that are absent from the decision-making process? Leaders in the community believe there is an opportunity for B Corps to learn from one another about inclusive legislation, policy, and communication practices.

Increased Collaboration with Other Community Groups

Many community groups are doing incredible work around brown/black solidarity. However, these groups are not necessarily working in the context of business. We believe there is an opportunity for B Corps to collaborate more with faith, activist, and other community groups.

Community Composition and Power Dynamics

It is clear that everyone in the B Corp community wants our movement to be more diverse. In particular, racial and ethnic diversity is a top priority for many B Corps. And although there is good gender parity in the community, this is primarily related to cisgender women and men. In the future, there is a growing interest in highlighting more stories about the experiences that gender-non-conforming and LGBTQIA individuals, people of color, immigrants, people with different abilities, and low-income individuals have had as part of the B Corp community. This could help put our movement on the radar of a wider group of people.

In addition to including a diverse group of people, we must closely examine the power dynamics of our community. Who is leading? Who is making decisions? Whose voices are heard more often? The B Corp community is already taking steps in this direction. Let's continue to push forward.

Insights from B Lab's Journey

Gleaning insight into what other people are trying can be a helpful aspect of this journey. This insight can shake things up, help spark new ideas, and reinvigorate your desire to make progress on the path. With that in mind, Jay Coen Gilbert, one of the cofounders of B Lab, has agreed to let us adapt an excerpt from the foreword he wrote for *Erasing Institutional Bias* (one of Dr. Jana's other books). In this piece, Coen Gilbert is very vulnerable and transparent about B Lab's journey of deeply examining DEI at its own organization.

> The words hit me like a punch to the gut, but they shouldn't have surprised me: "Only 57 percent of B Lab's staff who are people of color feel they can bring their whole selves to work, compared with 96 percent of their white coworkers."

> As a person who cares deeply about equity, I have spent considerable time and resources and dedicated my professional and civic life for the last decade to building a more equitable society and a more inclusive economy, so reading this statistic from a recent staff survey devastated me. It also shouldn't have surprised me.

> B Lab, an organization of roughly 65 people, is 68 percent white—whiter than the U.S. population, which according to the 2016 estimates by the U.S. Census Bureau is 61 percent non-Hispanic white. That wasn't what surprised me. What surprised me was that the staff survey suggested that our culture was more like 98 percent white. More specifically, white middle- to upper-class culture. I learned that there were things I never noticed that were negatively impacting our team's experience at work.

> For example, our primary office location is in a largely white, affluent suburb of Philadelphia, and that has created an unwelcoming environment for some team members. Other issues seemed to stem from economic and class disparities as well as the interconnected issue of race: our expense reimbursement policy assumes that our colleagues have credit cards and is ignorant of the fact that some who do have credit cards might struggle if we reimburse them after they need to pay their monthly bills. (This is more burdensome for some, given research that suggests that credit terms are often worse for people of color than for white people.) Personal sharing at our weekly staff meeting, intended to build connection and community, often features photos from a team member's amazing travel experience or beautiful wedding, which for some had a "must be nice for you," dissonant ring. General office chatter—whether in the kitchen, on Slack, or on GoToMeeting—reflects the life experiences, interests, and digital feeds of our team, and if that team is largely white and privileged, then just being around the office can be a daily reminder of "otherness" and an obstacle for some to bring their whole selves to work every day.

One staff member of color shared how difficult it was to be at work all day and endure a deafening silence among their colleagues about a police shooting of an unarmed black man the day before; the contrast between how the shooting had impacted their personal network and their work network was stark and uncomfortable.

Compounding these issues, B Lab has almost no people of color in leadership positions, creating a lack of role models for career development and contributing to a sense of isolation. It shouldn't have been surprising to learn that only 29 percent of people of color at B Lab said that there were role models they could relate to at B Lab, compared with 79 percent of their white peers. Perhaps all of these issues help explain why only 50 percent of people of color at B Lab felt that their social interactions at work were "good or great" (versus "poor or fair"), compared with 92 percent of their White peers.

Many often-intersecting types of bias—including occupational, class, gender, racial, and hiring/advancement bias, or bias against certain types of customers—can manifest in the workplace. One that has felt most pressing for B Lab, and for me personally, has been our implicit bias in hiring and advancement.

If a noninclusive culture, and bias, is more likely to persist in a homogenous culture, then a necessary step in building an inclusive culture and eradicating institutional bias is to build a more heterogeneous culture. That means diversifying the team at all levels to ensure that more heterogeneous experiences and perspectives can show up in the everyday interactions that create culture and can add value to solving problems and seizing opportunities that create great organizations.

In my experience, building a more diverse and inclusive workplace is often easier said than done. Here's one reason: we all tend to exist within networks that resemble ourselves. For example, according to research by the Public Religion Research Institute, 75 percent of white people do not have a significant relationship with a person or family of color. As a result, building racially heterogeneous teams and cultures requires commitment to getting out of our comfortable networks and patterns of behavior.

At B Lab, our biggest obstacle has not been intention; it has been commitment. Like many organizations, whether for-profit or nonprofit, the team at B Lab is running hard all the time. For every team member, there is always way more to do in a day, a week, a month, than they can do. As my partner likes to say, we will always be over-opportunitied and underresourced. In an environment like this, every person's understandable reflex, when filling open positions, is to fill them fast, to get someone talented and aligned on board ASAP. Faster if possible.

As a result, we too often have valued a speedy hiring decision over a strategic hiring decision. That often means we have filled full-time positions with interns—easily accessible, known quantities who have demonstrated they can do the work and are a "good cultural fit." And they can start tomorrow. At one point, roughly one-third of all B Lab staff were former interns.

As is the case in many organizations, however, interns often come from our personal networks—the schools we attended, a neighbor or colleague's children, or just local talent. For an organization like B Lab, with primary offices located in a largely white, affluent suburb, cofounded by three white people, this means our interns have looked almost entirely like us. And because we have often promoted from within, this desired internal upward mobility has had the unintended effect of maintaining a homogenous leadership and culture, as former interns rose into management and new interns joined us from the same old social networks.

As I reflected on how I might be creating or perpetuating institutional bias at B Lab, I realized I have personally exacerbated our difficulties in building an inclusive and diverse team by creating and perpetuating a culture that prioritizes speed over strategy. I work fast and long hours, creating expectations for the same, and my creative energy can turn safe-to-try ideas into dangerous-to-implement initiatives that overburden an already overstretched team. My pace, when coupled with my position of power and a lack of adequate self-restraint, has too often pushed us to hire faster, not smarter, as people understandably grasp for the nearest life preserver to carry them through the next set of waves.

This is at least one way I need to change my behavior to support the team in achieving our shared objective of building an inclusive, diverse, and best-in-class organization. Hiring outside of our existing personal and professional networks will require a sustained effort to identify partners, to explore areas of alignment, and to build trust. That will take time, and I need to change my behavior to create the space to make that possible.

A similar dynamic exists for building an inclusive, diverse B Corp community worthy of being called leaders. A community of business leaders cofounded by three white guys tends to beget more white guys. When building a community of business leaders (and society has created a situation in which most business leaders are white men), it's likely that, without explicit intention, commitment, time, and money focused on building a heterogeneous community, we are destined to get what we have got—a largely white, male community.

There are other factors at work, too, that have made progress more difficult. Despite the intention to diversify our community, many team members are limited in their knowledge of—let alone their relationship with—other professional networks serving underrepresented communities. Some may also feel reticent to lean in to build relationships with these networks, feeling unequipped—or even perhaps a little intimidated—to engage with, for example, communities of color about our work and how it may or may not resonate with their personal or business objectives.

As the staff survey illustrated, we have also been too slow to recognize the importance of inclusion in addition to the value of diversity. It is only recently, thanks to the thoughtfulness and advocacy of B Lab's Equity, Diversity, and Inclusion Committee, that we have spent time and resources creating more-inclusive event design and more-inclusive language and imagery in our marketing and communications. We have only just begun to think through the implications of the fact that women and entrepreneurs of color may have different needs and priorities that ought to shape the services and products we offer and that drive their particular value proposition for deciding whether it is worth the time, effort, and money to join the B Corp community.

For example, businesses led by women and people of color have a much harder time raising capital; they have more limited social networks of privilege, power, and resources; they are burdened with society-imposed biases that further limit their opportunities, which could be exacerbated if they are also seen by the gatekeepers to powerful business and investor networks as leading "less serious, do-good" businesses. All of these truths exist and make the reality of being a women-led or person of color–led business different than being a white-led—or especially a white male–led—business. With this understanding, we need to shape our offerings accordingly, and we are beginning to do so.

Although the efforts of B Lab and the B Corp community to lead by example have been slow and flawed, they have been real, despite the many challenges. We all have implicit bias and, as a result, so do our communities and our institutions. The B Corp community reflects the business community at large, and the business community reflects society. Hundreds of years of inequity have created a society in which only 3 percent of U.S. businesses with employees are owned by people of color and only 4 percent are owned by women. While 29 percent of U.S. businesses are owned by people of color, and 37 percent are owned by women, approximately 90 percent of businesses owned by people of color and by women are "solopreneurs," with no employees. Six percent of U.S. B Corps with employees are led by people of color and 23 percent are led by women. In a glass-half-full world, with regard to people of color– and women-led businesses with employees, the B Corp community is two times (for people of color) and nearly six times (for women) as diverse as the U.S. business community. In a glass-half-empty world, 6 percent and 23 percent are still unacceptably low, robbing our community and our society of the value that would be created for all of us by a more diverse community of leaders.

One of the most powerful things I have learned from Dr. Jana is the power in owning and naming the challenges we experience while turning our intentions into actions and our actions into results. This is especially true for white-led businesses and business communities, from which we too often hear either a deafening silence on these issues or which have the mistaken perception that institutional bias is a problem for "others," not for "us," a perception that prevents organizations and society from reaching their full potential. As Dr. Jana says, "We are all are part of the problem if we are participating in systems without questioning and leveraging our influence."

At this moment in history, we cannot afford to continue ignoring the inequities disproportionately affecting marginalized, vulnerable, and historically underrepresented communities. We can, and must, work individually, organizationally, and collectively as part of a deliberate, coordinated movement to dismantle the systems built by bias and to create a new normal of a purpose-driven, inclusive economy that works for everyone.

And Now, Over to You

If you are feeling overwhelmed, depressed, or saddened by the amount of work that still needs to be done, we get it. This journey is often physically and emotionally taxing. Yvon Chouinard once said, "Living the examined life is a pain in the ass." We tend to agree.

Ryan, Dr. Jana, and many of the others with whom we have spoken have taken solace in the deep connections, feelings of gratitude, and collective power of being on a shared journey with so many interesting and caring people. Even though we are all struggling to create a more diverse, equitable, and inclusive economy, being part of the B Corp community—being part of a global movement of leaders who are using business as a force for good—helps motivate us to continue to show up to work every day.

You may be wondering what's next. Now that you've finished this book, the first step toward measuring what matters, building a more inclusive business, and/or becoming a Certified B Corporation is to take the B Impact Assessment. If you haven't already, we recommend giving the assessment a try and telling your friends, family, and colleagues about this free tool that can benchmark their companies' social and environmental performance. If you want to learn how to build a more inclusive business, check out the book *Erasing Institutional Bias*, by Dr. Tiffany Jana and Ashley Diaz Mejias. We also strongly suggest checking out the inclusive economy best practice guides put together by B Lab. If you need inspiration, tips, or free templates to help you improve your score on the B Impact Assessment, sign up for LIFT Economy's monthly newsletter.[2]

We'll leave you with one of our favorite quotes, from Paul Hawken, environmentalist, entrepreneur, and author of *Drawdown: The Most Comprehensive Plan Ever Proposed to Reverse Global Warming*. We think his statement captures what we are collectively trying to achieve: "When asked if I am pessimistic or optimistic about the future, my answer is always the same: If you look at the science about what is happening on earth and aren't pessimistic, you don't understand the data. But if you meet the people who are working to restore this earth and improve the lives of others, and you aren't optimistic, you haven't got a pulse. What I see everywhere in the world are ordinary people willing to confront despair, power, and incalculable odds in order to restore some semblance of grace, justice, and beauty to this world."[3]

We hope that you have enjoyed this book and have found it useful. If so, please spread the word. If you have questions or comments, you can contact Ryan or Dr. Jana directly.[4]

APPENDIX A

Certified B Corporations and Benefit Corporations

What is the difference between a Certified B Corporation and a benefit corporation?

Certified B Corporations and benefit corporations are often, and understandably, confused. They share much in common but have a few important differences, as shown in the following table.

Comparison of Certified B Corporations and Benefit Corporations

Requirement	Certified B Corporations	Benefit Corporations
Accountability	Directors required to consider impact on all stakeholders	Same as Certified B Corporations
Transparency	Company must publish a public report assessing its overall impact against a third-party standard	Same as Certified B Corporations[a]
Performance	Must achieve a minimum verified score of 80 on the B Impact Assessment. Recertification required every three years against an evolving standard.	Self-reported
Availability	Available to any for-profit business in the world	Available only in specific countries (Colombia and Italy) and specific U.S. states (currently thirty-five states, plus Washington, DC, and Puerto Rico) that have passed benefit corporation legislation
Cost	Annual B Corp certification fees range from $500 to more than $50,000, depending on annual sales	Filing fees vary by jurisdiction. See benefitcorp.net for more information
Role of B Lab	Certifying body and supporting nonprofit behind the movement. Offers access to Certified B Corporation logo, portfolio of services, and global community of practice among B Corps.	Developed model legislation. Works for passage of benefit corporation legislation in new jurisdictions. Offers free reporting tool to meet transparency requirements. No role in oversight.

[a]Neither public reporting nor use of a third-party standard is currently required for Delaware benefit corporations. Details are available at bcorporation.net or benefitcorp.net.

Why was the benefit corporation legal structure created?

One of the primary challenges that the B Corp movement was created to address is the difficulty that many entrepreneurs have in raising capital, growing, or selling their business without diluting the company's original social and environmental values.

Through the leadership of B Lab and the community of Certified B Corporations, laws have been passed in several countries and in the majority of U.S. states to create a new type of corporation—the benefit corporation—that best meets the needs of entrepreneurs and investors seeking to use business to solve social and environmental problems while supporting sound financial performance. The benefit corporation is designed to help companies protect their mission through capital raises and leadership changes and gives entrepreneurs and directors more flexibility when evaluating potential sale and liquidity options. The legal requirement:

- give legal protection to directors and officers to consider the interests of all stakeholders, not just shareholders, when making decisions;
- creates additional rights for shareholders to hold directors and officers accountable to consider these interests; and
- limits these expanded rights to shareholders exclusively.

A more thorough discussion of the need for and rationale behind the benefit corporation, state-by-state instructions, and detailed technical information about benefit corporations is available at benefitcorp.net. The definitive book about benefit corporations is *Benefit Corporation Law and Governance: Pursuing Profit with Purpose*, by Frederick Alexander.

Do Certified B Corporations have to become benefit corporations?

It depends on your current legal structure and your location. Certified B Corporations are legally required to consider the impact of their decisions on all their stakeholders, as part of the terms of their certification. However, this does not necessarily mean that your company has to become a benefit corporation in order to meet the legal requirement. The legal requirement can be fulfilled through a variety of structures, including limited liability companies, limited liability partnerships, low-profit limited liability companies, cooperatives, sole proprietorships, and more. For example, Ryan's old company, Honeyman Sustainability Consulting, was an LLC. After successfully achieving B Corp certification, Ryan had to amend his LLC's governing documents to include language that required his business to consider all of his stakeholders when making decisions.

If your company is a corporation and you are based inside one of the jurisdictions that has passed benefit corporation legislation (currently thirty-five U.S. states, as well as Washington DC, Puerto Rico, Italy, and Colombia), then you would be required to reincorporate as a benefit corporation. For example, Patagonia is incorporated in California. California is one of the thirty-five states that has passed benefit corporation legislation. Patagonia had to reincorporate as a California benefit corporation in order to retain its B Corp certification.

If your company is a corporation and you are based outside any of the aforementioned jurisdictions that have passed legislation, then it is not yet possible to incorporate as a benefit corporation. For example, Small Giants is a company based in Australia. As of this writing, the benefit corporation legal structure is not available in Australia. In order to meet the legal requirement to become a Certified B Corporation, Small Giants signed an agreement with B Lab that, among other things, committed it to considering the impact of its operations on all of its stakeholders to the maximum extent permissible under Australian law. The agreement also stated that, in the event that benefit corporation legislation is established in Australia, Small Giants would be required to become a benefit corporation in order to retain its B Corp certification.

Regardless of your specific situation, B Lab acknowledges that changing corporate structure or articles takes time. B Lab allows a grace period for companies to complete the legal requirement after B Corp certification is complete. The length of this grace period varies depending on structure and location. See bcorporation.net for more details.

Do benefit corporations have to become Certified B Corporations?

No. Companies that are benefit corporations are not required to become Certified B Corporations. In fact, there are more than three times as many benefit corporations as Certified B Corporations in the world. For example, *This American Life*, the popular radio show in the United States (which also spun off *Serial* and *S-Town*, two incredibly successful podcast series), is a relatively well-known company that is a benefit corporation but not a Certified B Corporation. Some benefit corporations (like Patagonia, Kickstarter, and many others) choose to become Certified B Corporations because they want the added third-party verification of their social and environmental performance. However, this is not a requirement of becoming a benefit corporation.

Will becoming a benefit corporation affect my tax status?

In the United States, becoming a benefit corporation will not affect your company's tax status. Your company can still elect to be taxed as a C corp or S corp.

Benefit corporation status affects only corporate purpose, accountability, and transparency requirements. Everything else remains the same. Check benefitcorp. net for details on how benefit corporation laws work in other countries.

Aren't companies such as Aveda already socially and environmentally responsible without a benefit corporation legal structure?
Companies such as Aveda, Ben & Jerry's, Burt's Bees, and Tom's of Maine proved that one can run a profitable business and have a social mission. However, in times of crisis, such as the 2007 financial collapse, or under a leadership change, social and environmental values can get pushed aside if they are not embedded in the company's foundational documents. The benefit corporation legal structure provides entrepreneurs, owners, and investors with the assurance that the company's social and environmental values will remain equally important to making a profit—no matter what. For a good example of this, see the discussion of Whole Foods Market in part 2 of this book, in the section "Protecting a Company's Mission for the Long Term."

Perhaps most importantly, the highest court in the United States likely to decide any litigation around this issue also agrees. Leo E. Strine Jr., the chief justice of the Supreme Court of Delaware, wrote in 2015:

> There is a tendency among those who believe that corporations should be more socially responsible to . . . pretend that corporate directors do not have an obligation under Delaware corporate law to make stockholder welfare the sole end of corporate governance within the limits of their legal discretion. . . .
>
> According to these commentators, if only corporate directors recognized that the stockholders are just one of many ends they can legally pursue, the world would be a better place. Corporate directors, under this rosy view, may consider any or all of the following to be ends as important or even more important than the economic well-being of the corporation's stockholders: the employees, the customers of the corporation, the environment, charitable causes, the communities within which the corporation operates, and society generally.
>
> These well-meaning commentators, of course, ignore certain structural features of corporation law . . .
>
> It is inconsistent with judge-made common law of corporations in Delaware . . .
>
> Lecturing others to do the right thing without acknowledging the rules that apply to their behavior, and the actual power dynamics to

which they are subject, is not a responsible path to social progress. Rather, it provides an excuse for avoiding the tougher policy challenges that must be overcome if we are to ensure that for-profit corporations are vehicles for responsible, sustainable, long-term wealth creation....

If we believe that other constituencies should be given more protection within corporation law itself, then statutes should be adopted giving them enforceable rights that they can wield. The benefit corporation is a modest, but genuine, example of that kind of step forward.[1]

Have any companies lost their B Corp certification for not meeting the legal requirement?

Yes. Etsy, the Honest Company, and Warby Parker are good examples. Each of these companies was a Certified B Corp for more than five years. However, each company (for reasons beyond the scope of this book) decided against making the legal changes necessary before the required deadline to maintain their B Corp certification.

It was sad for the B Corp community—and perhaps sad for some of the employees of these companies themselves—to have them drop their B Corp status. In the end, however, B Lab made the right choice in not modifying or dropping the legal requirement to allow these companies and others to remain B Corps.

This has not been an easy process. B Lab is aware that the legal requirement is the single biggest impediment to the growth of the B Corp community. B Lab made a long-term bet. The bet is that sticking to the legal requirement, even though it makes the B Corp community grow much more slowly—and even though more well-known brands, like Etsy, the Honest Company, and Warby Parker, may have to drop out—is the best decision for the movement.

As Judge Leo Strine Jr. argues, and as the story of Whole Foods Market's acquisition by Amazon reveals, there is still a critical need for entrepreneurs and directors to have the legal protection to consider workers, community, and the environment, in addition to shareholders, when making decisions. Indeed, Laureate Education's successful IPO, Ripple Foods's ability to raise $100 million from mainstream investors, Danone North America's decision to become a public benefit corporation, and the growing number of publicly traded B Corps around the world all point to growing evidence that making the legal change to becoming a benefit corporation will be a nonissue in the future.

How do I become a benefit corporation?

It depends on where you are incorporated. If you are starting a new company in the United States, you can incorporate as a benefit corporation in any state where benefit corporation legislation has been passed. The procedure is nearly identical to that followed for any other corporate structure. If you have an existing company, you can elect to become a benefit corporation by amending your company's governing documents. You also can become a benefit corporation in a growing number of countries, such as Italy or Colombia. Visit benefitcorp.net for the most up-to-date information about your specific situation.

APPENDIX B

Sample Diversity, Equity, and Inclusion Surveys

The following sample DEI surveys are designed to provide your organization with enough information to begin (or restart) inclusion-focused work. We believe the DEI work should not be led by intuition or depend solely on a few experiential stories that instigated larger corporate action. Metrics enable leadership to gauge whether DEI concerns are isolated or widespread. The resulting data informs whether a DEI strategy needs to be narrowly focused or more comprehensive.

The following surveys are not comprehensive, but they do provide enough of a litmus test that you will have a concise, data-driven starting place for any strategy development that follows. TMI Consulting Inc. offers services to guide the process and interpret the results, and also offers more comprehensive assessments as well. We are providing two sample surveys here so that you can experience the types of questions you should be asking when considering DEI work. However, we do caution you to be careful with your data collection, interpretation, and dissemination of results. For professional assistance, please contact tmi@tmiconsultinginc.com and mention the *B Corp Handbook* DEI survey.

Leadership Structural Inclusion Survey

The Leadership Structural Inclusion survey will allow your leadership team the opportunity to examine some of the systems-level structures that either support inclusion or reinforce exclusion. These questions are only to be asked of executive leadership.

- Is the average compensation for men and women equal in comparable non-managerial and managerial roles?
- Do you have a standardized process to file employee complaints?
- Are employees taught how to file complaints?
- Does your organization have diversity and/or inclusion listed as a core value or as part of your mission statement?
- Does your organization have a diversity and inclusion strategy (a formalized directive that is intentionally occurring at the organizational level)?

- Does your organization have formal diversity and inclusion programs and policies?
- Does your organization have a diversity, equity, and inclusion council?
- Does your organization have employee resource groups with committees or boards whose objectives are clearly tied to the organization's business strategy?
- Does your organization offer talent development and mentorship with a culturally inclusive lens?

Employee Organizational Diversity, Equity, and Inclusion Survey

The employee organizational DEI survey can be administered to all employees and should be rated on a five-point Likert scale. Employees should respond with the extent to which they agree or disagree with each statement. For example, have employees respond with (1) strongly disagree, (2) disagree, (3) neither agree nor disagree, (4) agree, and (5) strongly agree.

- At work, I feel comfortable voicing my opinion in a group.
- The organization provides timely and accurate communication to all employees about policies, procedures, and expectations.
- The organization provides developmental opportunities for employees at all levels.
- The organization has a clear process for employee evaluation and feedback.
- Employees know and understand why the organization values diversity and inclusion.
- Employees of all ages and generations feel like valued members of the company.
- Employees of all races have similar experiences, opportunities for advancement, and access to resources.
- Employees feel welcome and respected in their work environments.
- Employees of all sexual orientations and genders—including gender-nonconforming—feel included.
- Employees feel they can bring their whole self to work and meetings.
- Employees with noticeable accents and people from foreign countries receive the same opportunities and access as their colleagues.

- Employees feel valued and included in decision-making processes.
- The organization provides an environment that allows employees to have a healthy work/life balance.
- Employees understand how to file a complaint.
- When an employee complaint is filed, it is taken seriously.

NOTES

Introduction

1. *Inc.* staff, *How a Business Can Change the World*, May 2011, http://www.inc.com/ magazine/20110501/how-a-business-can-change-the-world.html; Tina Rosenberg, "Ethical Businesses with a Better Bottom Line," *New York Times*, April 14, 2011, http://opinionator. blogs.nytimes.com/2011/04/14/ethical-businesses-with-a-better-bottom-line.

Part 1: Overview

1. Rick Alexander, "How Investors Really Feel About B Corps," B the Change blog, May 24, 2017, https://bthechange.com/how-investors-really-feel-about-b-corps-7dcf7988a6e3.

Part 2: Benefits of Becoming a B Corp

1. Goldman Sachs, *GS Sustain* (June 22, 2007): 21.

2. "Millennials in the Workforce: A Work–Life Integration," YPULSE, February 20, 2013, http://www.ypulse.com/post/view/millennials-in-the-workforce-work-life-integration; Lindsay Gellman and Rachel Feintzeig, "Social Seal of Approval Lures Talent," *Wall Street Journal*, November 12, 2013, https://www.wsj.com/articles/ social-seal-of-approval-lures-talent-1384304847.

3. Simon Sinek, "How Great Leaders Inspire Action," TED video, 18:04, from TEDxPuget Sound, September 2009, https://www.ted.com/talks/ simon_sinek_how_great_leaders_inspire_action.

4. Seth Godin, "Toward Zero Unemployment," *Seth's Blog*, March 27, 2013, http://sethgodin. typepad.com/seths_blog/2013/03/toward-zero-unemployment-.html.

5. bcorporation.net.

6. Goldman Sachs, *GS Sustain*, 21.

7. Jay Coen Gilbert, "Panera Bread CEO and Cofounder Ron Shaich Resigns to Join the Conscious Capitalism Movement," *Forbes*, December 15, 2017, https://www.forbes.com/sites/jaycoengilbert/2017/12/13/ boy-oh-boy-oh-boy-another-conscious-capitalist-joins-the-fight-against-short-termism.

8. "20 Moments from the Past 20 Years That Moved the Whole World Forward," *Fast Company*, May 2, 2017, https://www.fastcompany.com/3052958/20-moments-that-matter.

9. Elizabeth Gurdus, *Gap CEO Art Peck: Big Data Gives Us Major Advantages Over Competitors*, CNBC, April 11, 2018, https://www.cnbc.com/2018/04/11/gap-ceo-art-peck-big-data-gives-us-major-advantages-over-competitors.html.

10. You may follow the publication at medium.com and sign up for its free weekly newsletter at bthechange.com.

11. www.lifteconomy.com/podcast.

Part 3: The B Impact Assessment

1. See bimpactassessment.net.

2. Visit bcorporation.net to view the most recent fee structure.

3. Goldman Sachs, *GS Sustain* (June 22, 2007): 7, 47.

4. www.livingwage.mit.edu; www.livingwageforfamilies.ca/calculator; www.livingwage.org.uk/calculation; www.globallivingwage.org.

5. "Transgender-Inclusive Benefits: Questions Employers Should Ask," Human Rights Campaign, http://www.hrc.org/resources/transgender-inclusive-benefits-questions-employers-should-ask.

6. Hilary Rau and Joan C. Williams, "A Winning Parental Leave Policy Can Be Surprisingly Simple," *Harvard Business Review*, July 28, 2017, https://hbr.org/2017/07/a-winning-parental-leave-policy-can-be-surprisingly-simple.

7. Amy Richman, Diane Burrus, Lisa Buxbaum, Laurie Shannon, and Youme Yai, *Innovative Workplace Flexibility Options for Hourly Workers* (Washington, DC: Corporate Voices for Working Families, 2009), 16. http://cvworkingfamilies.org/images/CVWFflexreport-FINAL.pdf.

8. Stephen Miller, "Socially Responsible Funds Popular in Mission-Driven 401(k)s," Society for Human Resource Management, September 30, 2001, http://www.shrm.org/hrdisciplines/benefits/Articles/Pages/SRIfunds.aspx.

9. Heather Paulsen Consulting, "The Employee Benefit That Costs Employers Nothing and Provides Financial Security to Workers," B the Change blog, May 25, 2017, https://bthechange.com/the-employee-benefit-that-costs-employers-nothing-and-provides-financial-security-to-workers-92b69b7ff18e.

10. Daniel H. Pink, *Drive: The Surprising Truth About What Motivates Us* (New York: Riverhead, 2009); Amy Adkins, "What Millennials Want from Work and Life," Gallup Workplace, May 10, 2016, http://www.gallup.com/businessjournal/191435/millennials-work-life.aspx.

11. Cited in ERC, "Complete Guide to Training and Development," HR Insights Blog, January 30, 2014, https://www.yourerc.com/blog/post/Complete-Guide-to-Training-Development.aspx.

12. Leonard L. Berry, Ann M. Mirabito, and William B. Baun, "What's the Hard Return on Employee Wellness Programs?," *Harvard Business Review*, December 1, 2010, http://hbr.org/2010/12/whats-the-hard-return-on-employee-wellness-programs/ar/1.

13. Yvon Chouinard, *Let My People Go Surfing: The Education of a Reluctant Businessman* (New York: Penguin, 2006), 174.

14. Nikki Blacksmith and Jim Harter, "Majority of American Workers Not Engaged in Their Jobs," Gallup *News*, October 28, 2011, http://www.gallup.com/poll/150383/Majority-American-Workers-Not-Engaged-Jobs.aspx.

15. Jim Harter and Sangeeta Agrawal, "Actively Disengaged Workers and Jobless in Equally Poor Health," Gallup *News*, April 20, 2011, http://www.gallup.com/poll/147191/Actively-Disengaged-Workers-Jobless-Equally-Poor-Health.aspx; Blacksmith and Harter, "Majority of American Workers Not Engaged."

16. https://www.lifteconomy.com.

17. Sandrine Devillard, Sandra Sancier, Charlotte Werner, Ina Maller, and Cécile Kossoff, *Gender Diversity in Top Management: Moving Corporate Culture, Moving Boundaries*, McKinsey & Company, November 2013, https://www.mckinsey.com/~/media/mckinsey/business%20functions/organization/our%20insights/gender%20diversity%20in%20top%20management/gender%20diversity%20in%20top%20management.ashx;Credit Suisse, *Gender Diversity and Corporate Performance*, August 2012, https://publications.credit-suisse.com/tasks/render/file/index.cfm?fileid=88EC32A9-83E8-EB92-9D5A40FF69E66808.

18. Kirk Snyder, "Bringing the Outsiders In," *Guardian*, September 8, 2006, http://www.theguardian.com/money/2006/sep/09/gayfinance.careers.

19. Larry Fink, "Larry Fink's Annual Letter to CEOs: A Sense of Purpose," BlackRock, https://www.blackrock.com/corporate/investor-relations/larry-fink-ceo-letter.

20. 2020 Women on Boards, 2020 Gender Diversity Index: 2013 Key Findings.

21. Vivian Giang, "The Growing Business Of Detecting Unconscious Bias," *Fast Company*, May 5, 2015, http://www.fastcompany.com/3045899/hit-the-ground-running/the-growing-business-of-detecting-unconscious-bias.

22. P. R. Lockhart, "Tuesday Is Black Women's Equal Pay Day. Here's What You Should Know About the Gap," *Vox*, August 7, 2018, https://www.vox.com/identities/2018/8/7/17657416/black-womens-equal-pay-day-gender-racial-pay-gap.

23. Lawrence Mishel and Jessica Schieder, "CEO Pay Remains High Relative to the Pay of Typical Workers and High-Wage Earners," Economic Policy Institute, July 20, 2017, https://www.epi.org/publication/ceo-pay-remains-high-relative-to-the-pay-of-typical-workers-and-high-wage-earners.

24. Steven A. Rochlin and Brenda Christoffer, *Making the Business Case: Determining the Value of Corporate Community Involvement* (Boston: Center for Corporate Citizenship at Boston College, 2000), https://commdev.org/userfiles/files/750_file_making_the_business_case.pdf; Michael Tuffrey, *Good Companies, Better Employees* (London: Corporate Citizenship Company, 2003), https://corporate-citizenship.com/wp-content/uploads/Good-companies-better-employees.pdf.

25. Visit www.onepercentfortheplanet.org for more information.

26. www.lifteconomy.com.

27. Cohn & Wolfe, *From Transparency to Full Disclosure*, October 2013, 8.

28. bimpactassessment.net.

29. www.drawdown.org/solutions.

30. www.co2analytics.com; www.tripzero.com.

31. www.3degreesinc.com; www.nativeenergy.com.

32. Brian Carr, "Commute Options Programs Increase Employee Satisfaction, Retention," HR.com, November 3, 2011, http://www.hr.com/en/app/blog/2011/11/commute-options-programs-increase-employee-satisfa_gujwyz6m.html.

33. *Carbon Disclosure Project Study 2010: The Telepresence Revolution* (Carbon Disclosure Project, 2010). https://www.wwf.de/fileadmin/fm-wwf/Publikationen-PDF/Telepresence-Revolution-2010.pdf.

34. Robert Matthams, "Despite High Fuel Prices, Many Trucks Run Empty," *Christian Science Monitor*, February 25, 2012, https://www.csmonitor.com/Business/2012/0225/Despite-high-fuel-prices-many-trucks-run-empty.

35. David A. Carter, Betty J. Simkins, and W. Gary Simpson, "Corporate Governance, Board Diversity, and Firm Value," *Financial Review* 38 (2003): 33–53, https://www.researchgate.net/publication/4990531_Corporate_Governance_Board_Diversity_and_Firm_Value; Erica Hersh, "Why Diversity Matters: Women on Boards of Directors," Harvard T.H. Chan School of Public Health, July 21, 2016, https://www.hsph.harvard.edu/ecpe/why-diversity-matters-women-on-boards-of-directors/.

36. www.bcorporation.net or benefitcorp.net also can provide detailed information that is relevant to your specific situation.

37. Ramit Jain, Jehanzeb Noor, Janice Pai, Parag Patel, and David Ressa, "Supplier Quality Management: A Proactive and Collaborative Approach," McKinsey & Company, December 2012, https://www.mckinsey.com/practice-clients/operations/supplier-quality-management-a-proactive-and-collaborative-approach.

38. www.iso.org.

39. "NPS Pros and Cons: Why Use NPS?," SurveyMonkey, https://www.surveymonkey.com/mp/nps-pros-cons-why-use-nps/?ut_source1=mp&ut_source2=net_promoter_score_calculation; Adam Ramshaw, "Net Promoter Score Success Stories and Case Studies," Genroe, https://www.genroe.com/blog/net-promoter-score-success-stories-and-case-studies/984; "Net Promoter Score (NPS) Survey," SurveyMonkey, https://www.surveymonkey.com/mp/net-promoter-score.

40. Robert Hackett, "Data Breaches Now Cost $4 Million on Average," *Fortune*, June 15, 2016, http://fortune.com/2016/06/15/data-breach-cost-study-ibm.

Part 5: Conclusion

1. Robin DiAngelo, *White Fragility: Why It's So Hard for White People to Talk About Racism* (Boston: Beacon, 2018), 5. Emphasis in original.

2. See bcorporation.net/inclusion; www.lifteconomy.com/newsletter.

3. Paul Hawken, 2009 commencement address, University of Portland, May 3, 2009.

4. ryan@lifteconomy.com; tiffany@tmiconsultinginc.com.

Appendix A: Certified B Corporations and Benefit Corporations

1. Leo E. Strine, *The Dangers of Denial: The Need for a Clear-Eyed Understanding of the Power and Accountability Structure Established by the Delaware General Corporation Law*, University of Pennsylvania Law School Institute for Law and Economics, Research Paper no. 15-08, March 11, 2015. https://papers.ssrn.com/sol3/papers.cfm?abstract_id=2576389.

ACKNOWLEDGMENTS

Ryan Honeyman. I am forever grateful to the dozens of inspiring, loving, and supportive people who helped me write this book. In particular, I want to say thank you:

- to Dr. Tiffany Jana; you are amazing. This book would not have been possible without you.
- to the entire B Corp community; it is—and always was—about you.
- to the hundreds of B Corps who contributed their voices; your stories make this book come to life.
- to the entire B Lab team, especially Jay Coen Gilbert, Jocelyn Corbett, Dan Osusky, Jerrod Modica, and many others, who helped us complete this book.
- to all the people who read (and reread) our manuscript, including Diana Marie Lee, Jenny Kassan, Mike Hannigan, Rick Alexander, Vincent Stanley, Heather Paulsen, Josh Prigge, and many others.
- to my top-notch editor, Neal Maillet, and the entire team at Berrett-Koehler; your support, encouragement, and hard work were invaluable.
- to Zadie and Parker, my kids, for allowing me to work. Yes, I can now give you a ride on the blanket around the house.
- and finally, to my wife, whose unwavering love, support, and health insurance coverage (for the last six years and counting) made this book possible.

I could not have done it without any of you. Thank you!

Dr. Tiffany Jana. I would like to acknowledge my God, first and foremost. Through Him all things are possible, including this book. To my coauthor, Ryan Honeyman, for his patience, grace, and talent—and for inviting me along for this part of his journey. My parents, Gene and Deborah Egerton, for inspiring me to make a difference. Mom, thanks for showing me that you can use business as a force for good. Also, the fabulous Berrett-Koehler Publishing team has been an absolute dream to work with on this book as well as my other books, *Overcoming Bias* and *Erasing Institutional Bias*. Thank you to my mentors, friends, and family for encouraging me to be a unicorn on a mission.

INDEX

PHOTO CREDITS

p. 12: Photograph courtesy of Renata Thompson

p. 14: Photograph courtesy of B Lab Taiwan

p. 17: Photograph courtesy of Robert Bell Photography

p. 27: Photograph courtesy of ECO2Librium

p. 33: Photograph courtesy of Danone

p. 38: Photograph courtesy of B Lab East Africa

p. 42: Photograph courtesy of Small Giants

p. 44: Photograph courtesy of B Lab Europe

p. 45: Photograph courtesy of KK Tse

p. 50: Photograph courtesy of Ben & Jerry's

p. 52: Photograph courtesy of Mike Gifford

p. 56: Photograph courtesy of Mercado Birus

p. 67: Photograph courtesy of Cooperative Home Care Associates

p. 77: Photograph courtesy of Eileen Fisher

p. 85: Photograph courtesy of Sweet Livity

p. 95: Photograph courtesy of Jennifer Graham Photography

p. 103: Photograph courtesy of Maggi Woo

p. 113: Photograph courtesy of Beneficial State Bank

p. 121: Photograph courtesy of Felix Wilson

p. 126: Photograph courtesy of Sistema Biobolsa

p. 135: Photograph courtesy of Divine Chocolate

p. 143: Photograph courtesy of DOMI Earth

p. 152: Photograph courtesy of Animikii

p. 157: Photograph courtesy of Natura

p. 163: Photograph courtesy of Mike Roelos

p. 169: Photograph courtesy of Onnia Harris

p. 172: Photograph courtesy of B Lab Australia and New Zealand

p. 206: Photograph courtesy of Ryan Honeyman

p. 207: Photograph courtesy of Dr. Tiffany Jana

ABOUT THE AUTHORS

Ryan Honeyman is a partner and worker-owner at LIFT Economy. Ryan has helped more than thirty companies—including Patagonia, Ben & Jerry's, King Arthur Flour, and Native American Natural Foods—become Certified B Corporations, recertify as B Corps, and/or maximize the value of their B Corp certification. Along with his LIFT Economy team, Ryan helped cofound the Force for Good Fund (lifteconomy.com/forceforgood), a $1 million fund that invests in women- and people of color–owned, Best for the World B Corps. He is also a cohost of *Next Economy Now*, a podcast highlighting the leaders who are taking a regenerative, bioregional, democratic, transparent, and whole-systems approach to using business for good (lifteconomy.com/podcast). Ryan has been a featured speaker at SOCAP, Bioneers, the B Corp Champions Retreat, CatalystCreativ, the Social Enterprise Summit, and more. E-mail him at ryan@lifteconomy.com.

Dr. Tiffany Jana. The second edition of *The B Corp Handbook* is Dr. Jana's third book through Berrett-Koehler Publishers. Dr. Jana and their company, TMI Consulting, were featured in the first edition of the handbook, in 2014. They had the distinct pleasure of meeting *The B Corp Handbook*'s original author, Ryan Honeyman, at the annual gathering of B Corps—the B Champion's Retreat. The two hit it off instantly. Generally, any meeting of these two  coauthors yields peals of laughter emitting from one or both of them. Despite their shared love of levity, they share a deep concern for the well-being of the planet and the people on it. They both believe that conscientious business practices, as demonstrated through B Corp values and measured by the B Impact Assessment, can change our world for the better.

Dr. Jana is the founder and CEO of TMI Portfolio, a collection of socially responsible and interconnected companies working to advance more culturally inclusive and equitable workforces. An award-winning diversity practitioner and international public speaker, Dr. Jana has been featured in publications including *Psychology Today*, the *Huffington Post*, *Fast Company*, *MarketWatch*, and *Forbes*. They were also named an Inc.com Top 100 Leadership Speaker in 2018.

ABOUT LIFT ECONOMY

L IFT Economy is an impact consulting firm whose mission is to create, model, and share an inclusive and locally self-reliant economy that works for the benefit of all life. LIFT's vision is to completely transform the economy over the next five hundred years (although it is feasible to achieve this transformation in just a few decades). To grow this "Next Economy," LIFT works on projects like:

- **Consulting.** We help social entrepreneurs, investors, foundations, and other partners to enhance their social and environmental impact. [lifteconomy .com/services]

- **Next Economy MBA.** A business education for those who are interested in completely redesigning the economy for the benefit of all life. [lifteconomy .com/mba]

- **Investing.** The Force for Good Fund invests in women- and people of color–owned, Best for the World B Corporations. [lifteconomy.com/forceforgood]

- **Next Economy Now.** Subscribe to our weekly podcast featuring leaders who are using the power of business as a force for good. [lifteconomy.com /podcast]

- **Newsletter.** Sign up today for our free sixty-point business design checklist—plus monthly tips, advice, and resources to help you build the next economy. [lifteconomy.com/newsletter]

ABOUT TMI CONSULTING

TMI Consulting was founded in 2010 as a diversity and inclusion management consulting company. In 2012, the partnership merged with a diversity benefit corporation and a marketing LLC founded in 2003. TMI Consulting, Inc. was the first diversity focused B Corporation in the world and earned national and international recognition in the field of organizational development and civic engagement. Today, TMI Consulting continues to provide diversity and inclusion consulting services and works in partnership with the rest of the TMI Portfolio companies to provide a range of socially responsible, interconnected organizations working to advance cultural inclusivity.

TMI Consulting supports organizations of all sizes, locally, nationally, and internationally, in a variety of capacities. Our work is industry and sector agnostic. We work with for-profit corporations, nonprofits, churches, universities, foreign and domestic governments, and nongovernmental organizations.

We help organizations build cohesive, accountable, diverse, inclusive, and equitable workplaces. We offer a full suite of diversity and inclusion services, ranging from full-service, organization-wide assessment and strategic planning to keynotes and employee training.

Our keynote and training topics include Diversity, Equity, and Inclusion; Overcoming Unconscious Bias; Erasing Institutional Bias; Anti-Harassment and Anti-Discrimination; The Ethics of #MeToo in the Workplace; Social Entrepreneurship; Women in Leadership; and many more. Our team uses innovative technologies to engage audiences in dynamic assessments, training, team and community meetings, and seminars. Our curricula can be tailored to meet the needs of each client.

As a culture-focused organizational development consulting firm, we support organizations and communities across the United States and all over the world with some of their most challenging work. We are a values-driven company. Quality and integrity are critical to our business and we work hard to ensure that we deliver the highest level of service to all our clients.

As a Certified B Corporation, we have an ethical and legal commitment to providing a benefit to society. We measure our triple bottom line (profit, people, and planet) global impact using B Lab's B Impact Assessment. We've been named Best for the World in 2016 and 2018 for our social and environmental performance.

ABOUT B LAB

A historic global culture shift is under way to harness the power of business to help address society's greatest challenges. B Lab's goal is to accelerate this culture shift and make it meaningful and lasting. Our vision is that one day all companies will compete to be not just best *in* the world but also best *for* the world and that, as a result, society will enjoy a more shared and durable prosperity.

The business community can be part of the solution to global problems like wealth inequality, climate change, and social unrest. Through our network of global partner organizations and interrelated initiatives, B Lab works to create viable alternatives to an economic system that is failing to create these solutions.

B Lab's initiatives include B Corp Certification, administration of the B Impact Management programs and software, and advocacy for governance structures like the benefit corporation. Visit bcorporation.net for more details.

Powered by

More from Tiffany Jana

Overcoming Bias
Building Authentic Relationships across Differences
Tiffany Jana and Matthew Freeman

Control, conquer, and prevail!

Everybody's biased. The truth is, we all harbor unconscious assumptions that can get in the way of our good intentions and keep us from building authentic relationships with people different from ourselves. Tiffany Jana and Matthew Freeman use vivid stories and fun (yes, fun!) exercises and activities to help us reflect on our personal experiences and uncover how our hidden biases are formed. By becoming more self-aware, we can control knee-jerk reactions, conquer fears of the unknown, and prevail over closed-mindedness. In the end, Jana and Freeman's central message is that you are *not* the problem—but you can be the solution.

Paperback, ISBN 978-1-62656-725-2
PDF ebook, ISBN 978-1-62656-726-9
Epub ebook, ISBN 978-1-62656-727-6
Digital audio, ISBN 978-1-62656-729-0

Berrett–Koehler Publishers, Inc.
www.bkconnection.com

800.929.2929

Erasing Institutional Bias
How to Create Systemic Change for Organizational Inclusion

Tiffany Jana and Ashley Diaz Mejias

Inclusion through action!

All humans have biases, and as a result, so do the institutions we build. Internationally sought-after diversity consultant Tiffany Jana empowers readers to work against institutional bias no matter what their position is in an organization. Building on *Overcoming Bias*, which addressed individual and interpersonal bias, *Erasing Institutional Bias* scales up to foster change in organizations. Jana and coauthor Ashley Diaz Mejias bring together in-depth research on how biases become embedded into the workplace with practical and engaging tools that mobilize readers toward action. They confront persistent systemic biases—such as racism, sexism, hiring and advancement bias, and cultures of aggression—and offer solutions for controlling them. In a world divided, this book is designed to raise awareness about inequality and hold ourselves accountable for creating a world that works for everyone.

Paperback, ISBN 978-1-5230-9757-9
PDF ebook, ISBN 978-1-5230-9758-6
ePub ebook, ISBN 978-1-5230-9759-3
Digital audio, ISBN 978-1-5230-9761-6

Berrett–Koehler Publishers, Inc.
www.bkconnection.com

800.929.2929

More on Benefit Corporations

Benefit Corporation Law and Governance
Pursuing Profit with Purpose

Frederick H. Alexander

There is a new form of governance—the benefit corporation—that reorients corporations so that they work for the interests of all stakeholders, not just shareholders. There are already 5,000 benefit corporations in the United States, and venture capitalists, private equity firms, and institutions are beginning to invest. Distinguished corporate lawyer Frederick H. Alexander describes the stranglehold that shareholder primacy has on our current legal and financial systems. He then provides a comprehensive description of the alternative. Benefit corporations expand corporate purpose and extend the obligations of corporate managers to include the interests of all stakeholders. The book is an invaluable guide for legal and financial professionals, as well as interested entrepreneurs and investors who want to understand how purposeful corporate governance can be put into practice.

Hardcover, ISBN 978-1-5230-8358-9
PDF ebook, ISBN 978-1-5230-8359-6
ePub ebook, ISBN 978-1-5230-8360-2
Digital audio, ISBN 978-1-5230-8362-6

Berrett–Koehler Publishers, Inc.
www.bkconnection.com

800.929.2929

Dear reader,

Thank you for picking up this book and welcome to the worldwide BK community! You're joining a special group of people who have come together to create positive change in their lives, organizations, and communities.

What's BK all about?

Our mission is to connect people and ideas to create a world that works for all.

Why? Our communities, organizations, and lives get bogged down by old paradigms of self-interest, exclusion, hierarchy, and privilege. But we believe that can change. That's why we seek the leading experts on these challenges—and share their actionable ideas with you.

A welcome gift

To help you get started, we'd like to offer you a **free copy** of one of our bestselling ebooks:

www.bkconnection.com/welcome

When you claim your **free ebook**, you'll also be subscribed to our blog.

Our freshest insights

Access the best new tools and ideas for leaders at all levels on our blog at ideas.bkconnection.com.

Sincerely,

Your friends at Berrett-Koehler